30-MINUTE ITALIAN COOKBOOK

30-MINUTE

ITALIAN COOKBOOK

Classic Recipes Made Fast and Easy

FRANCESCA MONTILLO
Photography By Darren Muir

ROCKRIDGE
PRESS

For general information on our other products and services or to obtain technical support, please contact our Customer Care Department within the United States at (866) 744-2665, or outside the United States at (510) 253-0500.

Rockridge Press publishes its books in a variety of electronic and print formats. Some content that appears in print may not be available in electronic books, and vice versa.

Interior and Cover Designer: Patricia Fabricant
Art Producer: Meg Baggott
Editor: Rachelle Cihonski
Production Editor: Sigi Nacson
Production Manager: Riley Hoffman

Photography © 2021 Darren Muir.
Food styling by Yolanda Muir
Author photo courtesy of Wicked Shots Photography

ISBN: 978-1-63807-028-3
eBook 978-1-63807-143-3
R0

TO MY CLIENTS, BOTH IN MY COOKING
CLASSES AND ITALIAN CULINARY TOURS,
I LOOK FORWARD TO CONTINUING TO
COOK AND TRAVEL WITH YOU!

CONTENTS

INTRODUCTION ix

CHAPTER 1
FAST AND EASY ITALIAN COOKING 1

CHAPTER 2
HEARTY SOUPS AND SALADS 21

CHAPTER 3
PASTA, RISOTTO, AND POLENTA 37

CHAPTER 4
VEGETARIAN SIDES AND MAINS 59

CHAPTER 5
POULTRY AND MEAT MAINS 77

CHAPTER 6
SEAFOOD MAINS 93

CHAPTER 7
SWEET DRINKS AND DESSERTS 105

MEASUREMENT CONVERSIONS 117
RESOURCES 118
INDEX 120

INTRODUCTION

In 2015, I started a business called Lazy Italian Culinary Adventures. It was a lifelong dream of mine to start a unique business doing exactly the things I love—cooking Italian food, showing others how to do it, and traveling to Italy with eager students and Italy aficionados. But immediately, the name raised some eyebrows.

Everywhere I went, I was asked why I would call my business such a unique name, and occasionally I was asked why anyone would want to do business or associate with a person who has the word "lazy" in their business name. A business coach advised me to change the name, or failure would surely follow. What I was trying to accomplish was clearly lost in translation. But it was the legal name of the business, I liked it, and I wasn't going to change it.

So why the name? Well, as I told everyone, Efficient Italian Culinary Adventures just doesn't have the same ring to it! In fact, it's not about being lazy at all; it's about my cooking philosophy, which is all about being efficient in the kitchen. I love to cook—I really do. I grew up in Italy, where food and cooking were how we connected to one another; food brought us together. But what I don't love is being in the kitchen for hours on end, standing in front of the stove or kitchen island stirring, chopping, and prepping. Because even this Italian knows there's more to life than cooking and eating.

Since you're currently reading this book, I suspect we have similar sentiments. You like to cook, you like to eat, but what you don't like is spending hours in the kitchen in the name of a good meal. And with Italian cooking, you know—or you'll soon find out—that you don't have to. Italian food is about simplicity, great quality ingredients, smart use of specific products, and simple methods. Sure, there are dishes that require a laundry list of ingredients, hours in the kitchen, numerous steps and methods, and countless pots and pans. But this book isn't about those dishes. We will save those recipes for another time, another place.

In this book, you will find mostly recipes for full meals—with the exception of a few side dishes and a few sweet endings in the last chapter. These dishes take just 30 minutes from start to finish, including prepping and chopping ingredients and all the cooking. I'm being realistic and recognizing you have a life outside the kitchen—we all do. Cooking an authentic Italian meal should be part of your day, not your entire day.

I've included the Italian name for each dish, with the English translation, so when you're ready to travel to Italy, you can order versions of these dishes at Italian restaurants. Plus, when you post your beautiful dinner picture on social media, the Italian name will impress your friends even more! Many of the recipes include wine or antipasto pairing ideas to broaden your repertoire.

Are you ready to start cooking some delicious Italian dinners in 30 minutes or less? If so, *andiamo nella cucina*. Let's go to the kitchen!

CHAPTER 1

FAST AND EASY ITALIAN COOKING

Before we dive into the recipes, I would like to provide you with a bit of background on Italian culture, which very much revolves around food. After taking you on a virtual tour of Italy by describing its regional cuisines, I'll discuss the importance of various staples that you should have on hand to make your life in the kitchen much easier. Then I'll tell you about some kitchen utensils you'll need to guarantee a great final product. Some of these items are very basic, and you likely already have them; others will make great additions to your kitchen.

ITALIAN COOKING AND EATING CULTURE

It's no secret: Italians love to cook—and they love to eat just as much. Having been raised in Italy, I can attest that food is our most loyal companion. It's there for us in times of celebration, but also in times of sadness and grief. What do you bring someone who has recently suffered a loss? In Italy, we bring food.

I am often asked if I cook daily, and my answer is a resounding "yes!" And while most Italians cook at least one meal a day at home, many stay-at-home parents might cook three meals a day. Seasonality is also key in an Italian kitchen. Using seasonal ingredients is important for guaranteeing a more flavorful result. Fresh tomatoes are best in the summer, and sturdier vegetables grow best in the colder months.

Many of the recipes you'll find in this book are what Italians cook every day. But holidays are also centered around food. For example, *Il Cenone* is perhaps the biggest meal of the year and is served on Christmas Eve. Many families from southern Italy base their Christmas Eve menu on seafood, but others, especially in northern Italy, opt for big pasta bakes, like lasagna or baked ziti, along with cutlets, various meats, and lots of vegetable side dishes.

REGIONAL CUISINE

Italy is made up of 20 regions, and although some dishes may be eaten throughout the entire peninsula, others are very regional. Although I was born in the south and lived in Calabria for many years, I now lead food and wine tours all over Italy, so I have been exposed to the very different cuisines that make up Italian food. I have tried to represent many of the regions with the recipes in this book, while also introducing you to some dishes that are universally adored.

NORTHWEST

Valle d'Aosta, Liguria, Lombardy, and Piedmont are the regions of northwest Italy. The cuisine here is rich, buttery, and often creamy. Lombardy and its capital, Milan, enjoy wonderful risottos like Risotto Milanese (page 53), as well as dishes like Veal Milanese (page 88). Liguria is the birthplace of classic basil pesto, which is used in Pesto Pasta Salad (page 30). Also being on the coast, Ligurians appreciate great seafood. In Piedmont, mushrooms often find their way into the cuisine, especially in the fall and winter months.

NORTHEAST

The northeastern area of Italy consists of Emilia-Romagna, Friuli Venezia Giulia, Trentino-Alto Adige, and Veneto. Emilia-Romagna's capital, Bologna, is widely recognized as the birthplace of Italian cuisine, and the food here is decadent and sophisticated. All these regions enjoy egg pasta and stuffed pastas such as tortellini and ravioli. Tortellini in Broth (page 41) is based on a staple dish from the city of Bologna.

CENTRAL

Central Italy is home to Tuscany, Lazio, Le Marche, and Umbria. Here a wide selection of legumes, pastas, and meats are enjoyed. Tuscans are known as bean eaters and enjoy a variety of dishes that use them, such as Pasta and Bean Soup (page 25). Despite its name, Roman Egg Drop Soup (page 22) does not come from Rome but is closely linked to the cuisines of Lazio and Le Marche, while Chicken Saltimbocca with Cherry Tomatoes (page 81) does have its origins in Rome.

SOUTH

Moving on to the south, we have Abruzzo, Puglia, Basilicata, Calabria, Campania, and Molise. The food of the south has a kick. Peperoncino (red pepper flakes) find their way into many dishes. Produce is widely used in many courses, like Green Beans and Potato Mash (page 63) and Leccese-Style Sweet Peppers (page 61), a dish with origins in Puglia. Olive oil is the fat of choice. And because of its close proximity to the ocean, a wide selection of seafood is also served, such as Neapolitan-Style Cod (page 101).

ISLANDS

Away from the mainland we have Sicily and Sardinia, Italy's islands. Lighter in flavor, the cuisine of the islands is, not surprisingly, centered around seafood, like Spaghetti in Clam Sauce (page 50). Lots of produce and locally made cheeses are also very much enjoyed in these two regions. Southerners also eat a lot of produce, such as eggplant and zucchini. Similar to other southern regions, the islands make use of olive oil and peperoncino.

✺ A GUIDE TO QUICK ANTIPASTI ✺

Although this book is focused on 30-minute meals, a quick introduction to Italian cured meats and cheeses is in order, as these ingredients play such an important role in setting up an Italian table. They are mostly served as an antipasto, or foods that whet the appetite and get one started for the meal that is to follow.

MEATS: Prosciutto, soppressata, mortadella, pancetta, capocollo, oh my! These are just a few of Italy's most famous deli products. Thankfully, these items are readily available in the United States. You can find them in the deli section of most grocery stores. They should all be sliced very thin.

CHEESES: Cheeses make a great addition to any antipasto platter, and you certainly have a large selection to pick from, even in the United States. It's wonderful to select a few soft cheeses, as well as some hard ones. Mozzarella balls are delicious paired with prosciutto. A small bowl of fresh ricotta is great for dipping crostini or freshly cut veggies. Provolone is a standard in an antipasto plate; you can get it sliced, or cut the drier variety into cubes. Parmigiano-Reggiano and Pecorino Romano are both hard cheeses that pair wonderfully with the many types of meats found on an antipasto platter.

CRACKERS AND CROSTINI: You'll enjoy all the meats and cheeses much more with a few high-quality crackers and crostini to go along with them. And while a hint of rosemary or other Italian seasoning is welcomed, avoid overly complicated flavors in the crackers and crostini, so the flavors of the other main ingredients can really shine. A thinly sliced baguette works wonderfully.

PICKLES AND JARRED ITEMS: Olives, pickled artichoke hearts, Italian vinegar peppers, giardiniera (pickled mixed vegetables), and roasted red peppers are just a few of the items readily available at any large grocery store that will kick up your antipasto platter to an exciting new level. Often, you will see a wide selection of olives at a store's deli counter or olive bar. The other items can be found in jars on the shelves in the store's aisles.

NUTS, DRIED FRUIT, AND JAM: A mixed bowl of toasted hazelnuts, almonds, and pecans will make a great addition to your antipasto platter. You can also stuff dried figs with walnut halves to give them a bit of a flavor surprise. Fig jam will go nicely with the cheeses mentioned, or you can dip crostini into it.

SAMPLE COLD ANTIPASTO PLATTER

Creating an antipasto platter these days seems to be a true art form. Many people get stuck on how beautiful it must look, but that is not the most important part. Instead, select a balance of flavors and some contrasting textures. For example, soft cheese like ricotta will be wonderful on crunchy crackers. The saltiness of prosciutto is perfectly paired with the sweet, milky flavor of mozzarella. And briny bell peppers and artichoke hearts will be offset by the sweetness of dried figs. Adding grapes to a platter also offers some sweetness to offset some of the saltiness of the meats.

These items work very well together and make a great combination.

- Sliced and rolled-up prosciutto
- Sliced and folded soppressata
- Sliced or diced pancetta
- Mozzarella
- Ricotta
- Picked artichoke hearts
- Jarred roasted red peppers
- Dried figs
- Crostini

YOUR 30-MINUTE ITALIAN KITCHEN

An Italian dinner in 30 minutes? Yes, it can be done, and the recipes in this book will prove just how easy and delicious it can be! I emphasize fresh, high-quality ingredients, but there are ways to minimize the work and steps involved and make it easier on yourself.

It's about working smarter with the limited time we have. Perhaps that means multitasking or selecting boneless cuts of meats as opposed to large bone-in meats. It means stocking your refrigerator and pantry with the right ingredients, and arming yourself with a well-equipped kitchen. I'm not talking about rare ingredients used for just a few dishes, but multipurpose items you can use again and again. And the same goes for equipment. The items and ingredients I've listed here will serve you well, not just for the recipes in this book, but for many other dishes as well.

FRESH FLAVORS AND A FEW HIGH-QUALITY INGREDIENTS

Quality over quantity, that's Italy's culinary motto. Most everyday Italian recipes call for limited ingredients, maximizing each one's flavor profile. But while quality is key, Italian cooking isn't expensive. In the long run, you will end up using less of any given ingredient because each will be flavorful enough that you will not need much of it. I've provided you with an extensive list of high-quality ingredients that are easy to find at most large grocery stores in the United States; no need to go to a specialty Italian market for these items. I'll even point out *where* you can find them in the grocery store.

Many of these items are either widely imported from Italy, driving the cost down, or have US-made versions that are equally delicious. You'll note that I've maximized whole ingredients as much as possible, but there is no shame in using canned legumes, frozen vegetables, or canned tomatoes. Many Italians use these ingredients as well.

———— FRESH PRODUCE AND HERBS ————

❧ **BASIL:** A summery herb, basil goes particularly well with any dish that contains tomatoes. The large leaves bruise easily, and its peak freshness fades within a few days in the fridge. When summer rolls around and basil is abundant, I buy extra, and, along with parsley, wash, dry, and freeze it.

→ **BELL PEPPERS:** These come in all colors of the rainbow, but I find the red ones to be the most delicate and tender. They're great in sauces, as well as in classic dishes like Italian Sausages, Peppers, and Onions (page 85).

→ **GARLIC:** Garlic offers an almost peppery tone to most recipes and is great in seafood dishes. Garlic should be stored in a cool, dry place. A recipe may call for whole garlic cloves that are removed later or finely minced garlic that gets lost in the dish.

→ **MUSHROOMS:** How great are mushrooms in a 30-minute kitchen? My favorites are the ones with a gentler flavor profile, such as white button and cremini (aka baby bellas), which are the smaller cousins of portobello mushrooms.

→ **ONIONS:** Onions are another must-have in an Italian kitchen. You'll find many soups call for onions, as well as most risotto dishes. Store onions in a cool, dry place, and never in a sealed container, as they need to breathe.

→ **PARSLEY:** Another staple in Italian cuisine, fresh Italian flat-leaf parsley is used in countless dishes. This herb is an economical ingredient that adds a fresh flavor to any dish. It lasts just about a week in the fridge but can be frozen as well.

→ **TOMATOES:** Fresh tomatoes are best enjoyed raw, in salads or chopped up as a topping in bruschetta. But don't let an overripe tomato go to waste. Tomatoes past their prime are the perfect addition to soups and stews. While it's tempting to refrigerate fresh tomatoes, they should be stored on your counter, stem-side down.

→ **ZUCCHINI:** What I love about zucchini is how delicate they are, making them a great vegetable to use in a 30-minute kitchen. Zucchini cook very quickly, are great in soups, can make a tasty side dish, and are equally delicious simply sautéed with some garlic and olive oil. When buying zucchini, look for small ones, which have a more delicate flavor and fewer seeds.

MEATS, EGGS, AND DAIRY

→ **DELI MEATS:** Italians eat a lot of deli meats—in sandwiches, in antipasto plates, and sometimes added to pasta dishes. Plan carefully: Once sliced, they will remain fresh for only a few days. Or choose the vacuum-sealed versions, which will keep for several months in the refrigerator when unopened.

→ **EGGS:** Growing up in an Italian household, I frequently abstained from eating meat on Fridays. And while seafood was often the dinner of choice, I also ate a lot of eggs for dinner. With a few added ingredients, eggs aren't just a meal substitute, but a meal in themselves.

→ **FRESH MEAT AND POULTRY:** Meats of various types are always in my fridge and freezer. While boneless is my default most weeknights because it cooks faster, don't shy away from items such as pork chops or lamb chops, both of which cook in well under 30 minutes. Thinly cut chicken breasts, boneless thighs, turkey breast slices, veal cutlets, and various chops are also ideal in a 30-minute kitchen.

→ **PARMIGIANO-REGGIANO CHEESE:** Buy Parmigiano by the chunk and grate it as you need it. To be sure of its authenticity, check the rind. The real thing is branded with the name "Parmigiano-Reggiano" on it, so you should see part of the lettering on the rind. When you see a recipe in this book call for "grated Parmesan," you can be sure I am referring to the freshly grated version. If you are following a vegetarian diet, seek out a US-made Parmesan (see note under Pecorino Romano Cheese).

→ **PECORINO ROMANO CHEESE:** Made from sheep's milk, Pecorino Romano is sharper than its cow-milk counterpart, Parmigiano. A great choice to top pastas, soups, and even stews, Romano should also be purchased by the chunk and grated as needed. Wrap the chunk in plastic wrap, then add a layer of aluminum foil around it to keep it from drying out. Please note that neither Italian-made Parmigiano nor Romano is suitable for those following a vegetarian diet because of the animal rennet used in their preparation. There are several US-made brands that do not use animal rennet, such as Stella, BelGioioso, Whole Foods brands, Trader Joe brands, and Boar's Head, to name just a few. For recipes in the vegetarian chapter that sometimes call for grated cheese, we've opted to use ground nuts instead; feel free to substitute vegetarian cheese, if you wish.

→ **RICOTTA CHEESE:** Ricotta is a wonderful fresh cheese made from the whey left behind when other cheeses are made. In Italy, you will find it made from sheep's, cow's, or goat's milk, but in the United States it's mostly made from cow's milk. Being a soft cheese, it's wonderful as a spread on bread or added in a small bowl to an antipasto platter. It's also a key ingredient in dishes such as Pasta alla Norma (page 72).

→ **SAUSAGES:** Sausages offer a lot of flavor for the amount of time they take to cook. They are great added to sauces for a first course, and with vegetables they make a wonderful option for a second course. (In Italy, a second course usually consists of meat, seafood, or a substantial vegetable dish.) One item that is growing in popularity is precooked sausages. Al Fresco is my preferred brand. These are great in frittatas, in soups, or simply sautéed with some mushrooms and onions.

➻ **SEAFOOD:** Seafood lends itself well to the 30-minute kitchen, as most seafood cooks in well under that time. Seafood is a great main course, or with added pasta it easily turns into a two-course meal. Look for fresh seafood whenever possible, but you can also find high-quality frozen seafood.

➻ **SHREDDED MOZZARELLA CHEESE:** Well-known as a topping for pizza, shredded mozzarella has far more uses. A key ingredient in baked dishes, it's also the perfect addition to frittatas and can be sprinkled on top of some salads.

❧ IF YOU BOUGHT TOO MUCH . . . ❧

Fresh herbs freeze amazingly well, and I always have some staples, such as parsley and basil, in the freezer. Wash the herb first and pat dry with paper towel, then place it in a freezer bag and freeze for later use. Most vegetables also freeze very well. The key is making sure they are fully dry before they make their way into the freezer. As for meats, family-size packs are often cheaper to buy. When you bring them home, separate them into appropriate serving sizes for your family, pack in freezer bags, then freeze.

PASTA AND GRAINS

➻ **BREADCRUMBS:** Breadcrumbs used to be considered the poor person's version of Parmesan cheese. Added as a topping to many pasta dishes, they are now an integral component for preparing cutlets or anything au gratin. Breadcrumbs can be stored in the fridge or pantry; refrigeration will extend their freshness. I prefer freshly made breadcrumbs, which you can find in some bakeries, rather than the shelf-stable kind found in cardboard containers.

- **DRIED PASTA AND PASTINA:** Italians eat pasta just about every day. But even if you're not looking to add pasta to your daily menu, be sure to have a number of boxes on hand. Choose a variety of shapes and sizes to mix things up a bit. Pastina is dried pasta's little cousin. Essentially, *pastina* means "small pasta," and it comes in many shapes and dimensions of "small"—from teeny tiny acini di pepe to the larger though still very small farfalle. Pastina is perfect in soups and stews and can be cooked directly in the stock—no separate pot required.

- **INSTANT POLENTA:** Polenta makes a great gluten-free first course, especially in the fall and winter months when we're all craving added warmth. Polenta is often served with mushrooms (see Polenta with Sautéed Mushrooms, page 56) or sausages (see Polenta with Sausage and Peppers, page 55). The instant variety cooks in well under 30 minutes.

- **RICE:** Naturally gluten-free, rice is wonderful to have on hand for risottos and soups. Arborio rice is a starchy short-grain rice that's ideal for risottos, as it will give you a creamier final product. You can use less expensive long-grain rice for soups.

CANNED AND JARRED ITEMS

- **ANCHOVIES:** A staple in southern Italian cuisine, anchovies add a kick to any dish, without much added cost. When cooked in a recipe, they often melt into the sauce, leaving behind a savory flavor without any distinguishable fishy component. Use salt judiciously when adding anchovies, as they are often very salty.

- **ARTICHOKE HEARTS:** Great in antipasti, pasta salads, or chicken dishes, a jar or two of artichoke hearts are always in my pantry. Some come packed in olive oil, and some are prepared with brine. I tend to use the oil-packed ones in various dishes and keep the oil they come packed in, but I rinse off the brined ones, as they can be a bit too vinegary.

- **BEANS AND CHICKPEAS:** Canned beans and chickpeas are the perfect staple to add to a 30-minute kitchen. They should always be drained and rinsed under cold water for a few minutes to remove any extra sodium. Great in soups and salads, and a staple in the classic dish Pasta and Bean Soup (page 25), canned beans and chickpeas require very little cooking time. My preferred brand is Progresso.

- **CANNED CRUSHED AND DICED TOMATOES:** Crushed tomatoes are great in red sauces. My preferred brands include Pastene, Muir Glen, and San Marzano. Most come in 28-ounce cans, which makes the perfect amount of sauce for one pound of pasta. I tend to use crushed far more than whole or diced, as they are very versatile and save me the work of having to dice or puree them myself. Diced tomatoes are perfect for soups and stews and when you need a chunkier sauce. Muir Glen is a wonderful option, and so is the less expensive and easily found Hunt's. Most come in 14.5-ounce cans, which is the perfect amount to add to a large pot of soup. Any leftover canned tomatoes should be removed from the can, placed in a glass jar, and refrigerated for later use.

- **CANNED WHOLE PEELED TOMATOES:** Wonderfully juicy and delicious, whole peeled tomatoes add a depth of flavor to all soups, stews, and sauces. Some of my preferred brands include Pastene, Cento, Muir Glen, and DeLallo. More often than not, you will want to break them down into smaller pieces, or puree them completely. For a smoother sauce, add them to a blender and pulse for a few minutes.

- **ITALIAN TUNA PACKED IN OIL:** I am never without Italian tuna packed in olive oil in my pantry to add to salads, sauces, and pasta dishes. My preferred brands include Pastene and Genova, but StarKist also makes it and may be more readily available where you live.

- **OLIVES:** Olives are a staple in southern Italian cuisine and are often added to sauces and seafood dishes. Rinse olives before adding them to your dish, as the brine can be overpowering and can easily take over the entire dish.

- **ROASTED RED PEPPERS:** Red peppers in jars are a great addition to antipasti, salads, and even frittatas. The brine can sometimes be overpowering, so I typically rinse the peppers under cold water before using.

FROZEN FOODS

- **ITALIAN GREEN BEANS:** Green beans are a summer staple of Italian cuisine. You will always find the frozen variety in the grocery store, and they cook so much faster than fresh ones. Birds Eye, River Valley, and Wegman's brands are all good. Green Beans and Potato Mash (page 63) is one of my favorite dishes to prepare with frozen Italian green beans.

- **MIXED VEGETABLES:** Frozen mixed vegetables such as broccoli, cauliflower, and carrots are wonderful in dishes like Vegetable Minestrone (page 24). They cook faster than their fresh counterparts and are already cut, convenient, and picked at their peak of freshness—not to mention extremely affordable.

- **PEAS:** Ideal in simple dishes like Penne with Ham and Peas in Cream Sauce (page 44) or added to vegetable soups or risottos, peas are the perfect item to pick up in the frozen food aisle. They cook fast and are flavorful, and many kids also enjoy them.

- **SEAFOOD:** The seafood section is the most expensive section in any grocery store. While I prefer fresh seafood whenever possible, it's not always available. Frozen cod, tilapia, scallops, or shrimp can also be used in a pinch. Let them thaw out in the fridge overnight, or if you're in a hurry, place them in the fridge in a bowl of cold water for 2 to 3 hours for faster thawing.

- **STUFFED PASTA:** Frozen ravioli and tortellini are fine to use when paired with wonderful sauces in recipes such as Ravioli with Tomato-Basil Sauce (page 40) or Tortellini in Broth (page 41). These cook very fast—so fast, in fact, that I recommend watching them carefully, because they will easily overcook and break apart.

DRIED HERBS AND SPICES

- **BLACK PEPPER:** Ideal for seasoning many meats, black pepper is a staple in most cuisines. Buying an inexpensive grinder and grinding peppercorns as needed will give you optimal flavor.

- **BOUILLON CUBES:** Another indispensable item in my kitchen is large, soft bouillon cubes. My preferred brand is Knorr. I use them a lot and will often replace canned stock with them. They come in chicken, beef, seafood, and vegetable flavors. They are big, so when I need only a small amount of stock, I break one in half or into thirds.

- **ITALIAN DRIED HERB BLEND:** A good blend of Italian dried herbs will contain oregano, basil, parsley, rosemary, thyme, and sage. Rub the herbs between your fingers before using to release their natural oils.

- **OREGANO:** Oregano is perfect in all sorts of dishes, from chicken and pork to tomato sauces. It's particularly appropriate to use in seafood dishes, and you will find that a number of dishes in the seafood chapter call for oregano. Simply Organic makes a wonderfully flavorful dried oregano.

- ⤳ **PEPERONCINO (RED PEPPER FLAKES):** Used frequently in dishes from southern Italy and the islands, red pepper flakes should be used carefully and with a light hand. It's far too easy to go from perfect heat to an inedible dish.

- ⤳ **SEA SALT:** While you have many options, I find that a basic fine sea salt does the job for most dishes. In the recipes, I've listed most salt to taste, as everyone's salt tolerance is different. But when cooking pasta, I recommend 1 tablespoon of sea salt for every 1 pound of pasta, and at least 4 quarts of water in a 6-quart pot.

OIL AND VINEGAR

- ⤳ **BALSAMIC VINEGAR:** There's balsamic vinegar, and then there's Traditional Balsamic Vinegar of Modena. The traditional variety is made in only two specific areas of northern Italy: Modena and Reggio Emilia. Trebbiano and Lambrusco grapes are used, the vinegar is aged in oak barrels, and the older it is, the thicker and sweeter it gets. Of course, the price will match its authenticity. It's not practical to cook with the traditional variety because of the cost. Other vinegars labeled "balsamic" are processed, thinner, and made in numerous places all over the world. While not the traditional kind, the cost makes them a viable option for cooking. Look for balsamic vinegar without added coloring or caramel.

- ⤳ **EXTRA-VIRGIN OLIVE OIL:** EVOO is cold-pressed, meaning there is no heat used in making it. It's made by grinding olives into an olive paste, then pressing that paste between stones to extract the juice. The color is darker than regular olive oil, it's peppery, and it leaves a ting of spiciness at the back of the throat. I reserve EVOO for use in raw preparations, in salads, or over grilled meats. Monini, Colavita, and California Olive Ranch Everyday Extra-Virgin Olive Oil are all easy-to-find, reputable brands.

- ⤳ **OLIVE OIL:** Regular olive oil is a blend of EVOO and processed olive oil that has been heated. Any olive oil that doesn't make the cut to be labeled EVOO is turned into the regular variety. I often use regular olive oil in cooking. Filippo Berio, Whole Foods, and Wegman's Organic oil are all trustworthy brands.

- ⤳ **RED WINE VINEGAR:** The most common dressing for salads in Italy, red wine vinegar is a staple in southern Italian cooking. It's wonderful on any salad containing iceberg, romaine, or even escarole. Thinly sliced cucumbers dressed simply with a generous amount of red wine vinegar, a drizzle of EVOO, sea salt, and dried oregano is a Calabrian "digestive" salad, eaten at the end of a heavy meal to aid with digestion.

❧ WINE DOWN ❧

Think you have to spend hundreds on good Italian wine? Think again! Italians drink wine at just about every dinner, and you can rest assured they're not spending hundreds per bottle. Table wine, as Italians call it, is the type of wine you drink daily: the type that goes great with everything, isn't pretentious, and won't make you feel guilty if you use it in cooking. Here is a short list of a few varieties that will go well with a range of dishes, both in the preparation of a recipe and to enjoy with dinner.

WHITES

ASTI SPUMANTE: A fruity sparkling white, Asti is a cheaper version of Champagne. Rather than cooking with it, reserve this one to enjoy with baked goods, biscotti, or a slice of Christmas panettone bread. Mix in some peach puree and you have a homemade Bellini (see page 107).

SAUVIGNON BLANC: With fruity flavors of apples and peaches and high acidity, this is the wine to select if you want a more pronounced, full-flavored white. It pairs great with chicken and seafood and is even good as an aperitif with an antipasto platter.

PINOT GRIGIO: This is my go-to wine for cooking and drinking. It's dry and crisp, with hints of citrus. It's a great everyday wine that deserves to be enjoyed often, especially on a hot summer day. This perfect accompaniment to chicken, turkey, and seafood can be enjoyed with Chicken Piccata (page 80), Mixed Fish Fry (page 95), or great barbecue.

SOAVE: Less famous than the ever-popular Pinot Grigio, Soave is another wonderful option to pair with poultry and seafood. It has a bit more body than Pinot Grigio, with subtle fruity undertones. It's also a good selection to pair up with desserts, such as Warm Peaches with Chocolate and Crushed Amaretti (page 110).

KITCHEN EQUIPMENT

A well-equipped and organized kitchen is key to maximizing your time and efficiency at mealtimes. These are the basics any home cook should have—in addition to standard measuring cups and spoons. With the exception of a very few items, these need not be expensive. And any investment you make up front will be worthwhile in the long run, as this equipment will last you a long time.

- **COLANDER:** This is an iconic item in a country that eats pasta daily. A colander or two is an absolute must in any kitchen. Used to drain cooked vegetables and pasta, as well as rinse uncooked vegetables or fruits, colanders come in all shapes and sizes and are relatively inexpensive.

- **CUTTING BOARD:** I use a number of different cutting boards. Some are specifically for meats or seafood, others for fruits or vegetables. I use wood for produce, for slicing bread, and for hard cheeses and deli meats. The wood ones shouldn't go in the dishwasher, so for raw meat and seafood, I use a plastic one that can be sanitized in the heat of the dishwasher.

- **KNIVES:** Good knives are an investment, but with good care and proper sharpening, they will last a long time. The set should come in various sizes for various uses in the kitchen and at the table. Also consider purchasing a knife sharpener, or have the knives professionally sharpened as needed.

- **MIXING BOWLS:** These are some of my most-used kitchen items. I use them to wash produce and marinate any number of meats. I also place one underneath the colander when draining pasta or vegetables in case I need any of that water for the final dish. Stainless steel bowls will last a long time and are inexpensive.

- **PEELERS:** A good peeler will save you time in the kitchen. Some are better than others, so it has taken me a few purchases to find my favorite one (The Pioneer Woman from Walmart).

- **SAUTÉ PANS AND SKILLETS:** Sauté pans have flat bottoms and straight sides, making them the perfect tool when you will be cooking a large volume of ingredients. Buy one that is big enough to hold a pound of pasta and its sauce (many pasta dishes finish cooking directly in the sauce). Skillets are perfect for frying and browning, but they have flared edges, so a 12-inch skillet will actually only have about 10 inches of cooking surface. Use them for recipes with fewer ingredients and no liquid.

- **SHEET PANS:** While only a few recipes in this book require a sheet pan, having a few in the kitchen will prove to be very useful, especially for baking. They come in different sizes and materials and are inexpensive, and with some basic care and hand washing, they will last a long time.

- **SLOTTED AND WOODEN SPOONS:** I have more than 50 wooden spoons; Italians seem to have a fascination with them! I don't think you need nearly as many, but grab a set to keep on hand. They're inexpensive and, well, I have yet to cook anything that didn't require the use of a wooden spoon.

- **SOUP POT OR DUTCH OVEN:** Extremely versatile items, soup pots and Dutch ovens have multiple uses, from the obvious soups to pasta, vegetables, and stews. A few of these in the kitchen are all you need. I particularly like Dutch ovens. They conduct heat well, can go from stove to fridge to oven, and are practically indestructible.

KITCHEN TIME-SAVERS

Here are a few items that I think are nice to have but aren't necessarily a must in your kitchen. These are just items that make your life easier, but other tools could also be used to get the job done.

- **FOOD PROCESSOR:** For speed and efficiency in the kitchen, nothing replaces a trusted food processor. It chops vegetables, potatoes, nuts, and onions in record time. It's also great for making pestos of all sorts.

- **GARLIC PRESS:** If you're not a fan of garlicky fingers, this does an excellent job of mincing garlic extremely fine.

- **MANDOLINE:** I like a mandoline for finely slicing zucchini, eggplant, and potatoes. A good knife will also do this, but this method is faster and every slice is identical. It's probably one of the most dangerous tools in the kitchen! Always use the safety guard that comes with it.

❧ THERE ARE NO MISTAKES IN THE KITCHEN ❧

In teaching cooking classes, I am often asked, "Can I . . .?" What follows is usually a question about whether one can substitute an ingredient for another, or whether a different wine can be paired, or if a cooking method can be altered. My answer is usually, "Of course you can!" No recipe is written in stone. There are no "mistakes" in the kitchen, just experiences that teach you how to better cook a dish the next time. You can improvise along the way. In fact, if you're a novice in the kitchen, I highly encourage it. When you're cooking in your kitchen after a hard day's work, the goal is getting a delicious dinner on the table in minimal time, not achieving perfection.

ABOUT THE RECIPES

As the title of this book suggests, the recipes that follow will take you 30 minutes in total from start (prep) to finish (cooking). There's work, commuting, child-raising, pets, errands, chores, doctors' appointments, cleanup, and so much more in our daily lives. Add cooking to that, and I know you have a full plate—no pun intended! I am hoping you will find the recipes enticing, delicious, and inspiring enough to want to get in the kitchen.

A number of the recipes are my own take on classic and authentic Italian dishes you would see in homes and restaurants throughout Italy. I've altered a few ingredients or steps to either reduce the time to fit into our precious 30-minute window or to adapt to the fact that some ingredients may be harder to find in this country.

You'll note that there's an emphasis on fresh ingredients. But to maximize those 30 minutes, there will be times when we will use convenience items, such as frozen vegetables, canned beans, and canned tomatoes—because they're the perfect weeknight ingredients.

Multitasking is also emphasized in the recipes. When the pasta is cooking, we will take advantage of that valuable time to prepare the sauces or other ingredients used in the dish. We will use your time well to help you make these dishes in that promised 30-minute window.

LABELS

Almost all the recipes in this book have at least one of the following labels. These labels will make it easier to decide what to prepare. I've labeled the recipes so when you have to make a dinner decision quickly, you can look at them and see what best suits your mood and situation.

- ◆ **ONE POT OR ONE PAN** (cooking happens in one vessel, although one additional prep vessel may be called for)

- ◆ **5 INGREDIENTS OR FEWER** (not counting salt, pepper, oil, and water)

- ◆ **DAIRY-FREE**

- ◆ **GLUTEN-FREE**

- ◆ **NUT-FREE**

- ◆ **VEGETARIAN**

- ◆ **VEGAN** (in which case, the recipe will also be Vegetarian and Dairy-Free)

—— TIPS ——

You will also find useful tips at the end of most recipes. The tips will be a resource when you're wondering what to pair a recipe with or whether there's a shortcut you can take along the way. Some tips offer information about ingredients used in the recipe or suggest ways to mix things up a bit.

- ◆ **PAIRING TIP:** Wine and appetizers go well with just about any main course. This tip will guide you on what to best pair your dish with.

- ◆ **SHORTCUT:** Looking to cut even more time in the kitchen? These shortcuts will speed things up.

- ◆ **INGREDIENT TIP:** New to a particular ingredient? Here you'll find tips on selecting, preparing, or storing some less-familiar items.

- ◆ **VARIATION:** Small changes can go a long way. Look for this tip for ways to mix up a dish a bit or for advice on what you can use as a substitute.

CAPRESE-STYLE TORTELLINI SALAD, PAGE 31

CHAPTER 2

HEARTY SOUPS AND SALADS

Roman Egg Drop Soup | *Stracciatella alla Romana* 22

Tuscan Bread and Tomato Soup | *Pappa al Pomodoro* 23

Vegetable Minestrone | *Minestra di Verdure* 24

Pasta and Bean Soup | *Minestra di Pasta e Fagioli* 25

Tuscan Soup | *Acquacotta Toscana* 26

Mamma's Classic Pastina | *Pastina di Mamma* 27

Imperial Soup | *Zuppa Imperiale* 28

Panzanella | *Insalata Panzanella* 29

Pesto Pasta Salad | *Insalata di Pasta con Pesto* 30

Caprese-Style Tortellini Salad |
Insalata di Tortellini in Stile Caprese 31

Antipasto Salad | *Insalata Antipasto* 32

Italian Rice Salad | *Insalata di Riso* 34

ROMAN EGG DROP SOUP

◇◇◇◇◇◇◇◇◇◇◇◇◇ STRACCIATELLA ALLA ROMANA ◇◇◇◇◇◇◇◇◇◇◇◇◇

The word *stracciatella* means "little shreds" or "things that have been torn." One might say that the eggs in this soup look like little shreds, hence its name. This is a homey dish frequently prepared in Rome but recognized throughout the country. It's the perfect soup for a cold winter night. It's often prepared with freshly made stock, but using store-bought stock cuts down significantly on time. It's an old-fashioned dish that requires few ingredients, which you likely already have on hand.

SERVES 4
PREP TIME: 5 minutes
COOK TIME: 10 minutes

4 cups beef, chicken,
or vegetable stock

2 cups water

4 large eggs

¾ cup grated
Parmigiano-Reggiano or
Pecorino Romano cheese

Freshly ground black pepper

Sea salt

1 In a 2-quart pot, combine the stock and water. Cover and bring to a boil over high heat.

2 Meanwhile, in a medium bowl, use a fork to whisk together the eggs, cheese, and pepper.

3 Pour the egg mixture into the boiling stock and stir constantly for 30 to 45 seconds with a whisk. Continue cooking for 5 to 6 minutes, whisking occasionally when the eggs come to the top. You will start to see what looks like shreds of eggs.

4 Taste and season with pepper and salt as needed. Serve hot.

VARIATION: For a more filling soup, add some spinach to the boiling stock, or add some toasted breadcrumbs to the egg mixture before dropping it into the hot stock.

TUSCAN BREAD AND TOMATO SOUP

◇◇◇◇◇◇◇◇◇◇◇◇◇◇◇◇◇◇◇◇ PAPPA AL POMODORO ◇◇◇◇◇◇◇◇◇◇◇◇◇◇◇◇◇◇◇◇

Pappa al pomodoro is a classic Tuscan dish that makes use of day-old bread. In Italy, it's often prepared with passata, which is unseasoned pureed tomatoes; passata is not readily available here, so we're using canned crushed tomatoes. This soup is thicker than the tomato soup we're used to here in the United States, thanks to the addition of the bread. For a thinner soup, adjust the amount of water, as noted in the recipe. Depending on the bread you use, you can choose to remove the crust for a finer, less chunky soup.

SERVES 4
PREP TIME: 5 minutes
COOK TIME: 25 minutes

3 tablespoons olive oil, plus more for drizzling

½ small yellow or white onion, finely chopped

2 to 3 garlic cloves, minced

2 tablespoons chopped fresh parsley

2 tablespoons chopped fresh basil, plus more for garnish

Sea salt

Freshly ground black pepper

1 (28-ounce) can crushed tomatoes

2 cups water, plus more as needed

6 cups cubed day-old bread, crouton size

1 In a large saucepan, heat the oil over medium heat for 1 to 2 minutes. Add the onion, garlic, parsley, basil, and salt and pepper to taste. Cook for 2 minutes, or until the onion is slightly softened and the garlic is golden but not burned.

2 Carefully add the tomatoes—they will splatter as they hit the hot oil. Add the water and simmer over low heat for 6 to 7 minutes, until the soup has thickened slightly.

3 Add the bread cubes and stir, mixing and breaking the bread with a wooden spoon as it softens in the soup. Cook for 10 minutes, stirring occasionally as needed to break down the bread further. For a thinner soup, add 1 to 2 cups more water.

4 Taste and add more salt and pepper as needed. Serve hot with a drizzle of olive oil and some fresh basil on top.

PAIRING TIP: Since tomatoes are the main ingredient in this soup, it will pair perfectly with a glass of Sangiovese wine, which has enough acid to complement the acid in the tomatoes.

VEGETABLE MINESTRONE

◇◇◇◇◇◇◇◇◇◇◇◇◇◇◇◇◇◇◇ MINESTRA DI VERDURE ◇◇◇◇◇◇◇◇◇◇◇◇◇◇◇◇◇

There is nothing as comforting as a big bowl of vegetable minestrone on a cold winter day. It may have started in Italy, but this soup is now widely enjoyed here in the United States as well and is a popular choice on many Italian restaurant menus. While some versions of minestrone have a long cooking time, a combination of quick-cooking vegetables like the ones used here will have you enjoying a bowl of this hearty soup in no time. There's no *exact* recipe for this classic, so the vegetables used are all according to your preference.

SERVES 4 to 6
PREP TIME: 5 minutes
COOK TIME: 25 minutes

---

3 tablespoons olive oil

1 small yellow or white onion, diced

1 carrot, finely diced

1 tablespoon chopped fresh parsley

1 (14.5-ounce) can diced tomatoes

4 cups vegetable stock

2 cups water

1 pound frozen Italian vegetables

1 zucchini, cut into ¼-inch dice

1 (15-ounce) can cannellini beans, drained and rinsed

Sea salt

Freshly ground black pepper

1 (12-ounce) bag fresh spinach

1 In a large soup pot, combine the oil, onion, carrot, and parsley and cook over medium heat for 1 minute, or until the onion is slightly softened. Add the tomatoes, stir, and cook for 1 more minute.

2 Add the stock, water, frozen vegetables, zucchini, cannellini beans, and salt and pepper to taste. Increase the heat to high, cover, and cook for 15 minutes, stirring occasionally. If you want a brothier soup, add an additional cup of water.

3 Add the spinach and, using a wooden spoon, pack the leaves down into the hot soup. Continue cooking for about 2 minutes, or until the spinach is wilted. Serve hot.

VARIATION: To make this dish even more filling, add some pastina, such as ditalini. Check the cooking time on the package and add it during the last 5 to 7 minutes of the soup's cooking time.

PASTA AND BEAN SOUP

◇◇◇◇◇◇◇◇◇◇◇◇◇◇ MINESTRA DI PASTA E FAGIOLI ◇◇◇◇◇◇◇◇◇◇◇◇◇◇

While this is a classic Italian dish, there are as many ways to prepare it as there are nonnas in Italy! Some serve it dry, some serve it very soupy, and some add lots of tomatoes, while others serve it *in bianco*, meaning without tomatoes. This version is one of the many ways I make it myself, depending on my mood and what's in the cupboard, but it's not written in stone. See the tip for variations.

SERVES 4
PREP TIME: 5 minutes
COOK TIME: 25 minutes

3 tablespoons olive oil

2 carrots, diced

½ small onion, diced

2 garlic cloves, minced

3 tablespoons chopped fresh parsley

1 cup canned crushed tomatoes

2 (15-ounce) cans cannellini beans, drained and rinsed

Sea salt

Water

8 ounces elbow macaroni or other small pasta

Grated Parmigiano-Reggiano cheese (optional)

1 In a large soup pot, combine the oil, carrots, onion, garlic, and parsley. Sauté over medium heat for about 2 minutes, or until the onion is slightly softened and the garlic is golden but not burned.

2 Add the crushed tomatoes and continue cooking for 2 minutes, or until it's simmering. Add the beans, salt to taste, and enough water so it comes several inches above all the ingredients. Bring to a full boil over high heat and cook for 6 minutes, stirring occasionally.

3 Add the pasta, stir, and cook according to the package directions (usually about 11 minutes), stirring occasionally.

4 Spoon into bowls. If desired, garnish with Parmigiano.

VARIATION: You can make this soup *in bianco* by skipping the tomatoes or by adding just 1 diced fresh tomato instead. You can also add chopped sausage or pancetta when you sauté the onion. Or, for a stew-like dish, rather than soup, cook the pasta separately and add it at the end. To do this, reduce the amount of water that gets added with the beans to just enough to cover the ingredients. Then cook the pasta separately in a pot of boiling water, drain, and stir into the soup after it's fully cooked.

TUSCAN SOUP

The literal translation of *acquacotta* is "cooked water," but there are a few more ingredients than that. This is a specialty of Tuscany, particularly of the area of Maremma, and it's considered part of the *cucina povera*, or "poor man's cooking." There is no exact recipe, so the one here uses common, easy-to-find ingredients. The one consistent ingredient in all versions is the eggs, which are added to the hot soup. They are a key component of this dish, so be sure to include them to keep it authentic.

SERVES 4
PREP TIME: 10 minutes
COOK TIME: 20 minutes

3 tablespoons olive oil

1 pint cherry tomatoes

1 small yellow or
white onion, diced

2 carrots, diced

2 celery stalks, diced

2 tablespoons chopped
fresh parsley

Sea salt

Freshly ground black pepper

4 cups vegetable stock

4 large eggs

4 thick slices Italian
bread, toasted

1 In a 3-quart sauté pan with sides at least 4 inches high, combine the oil, tomatoes, onion, carrots, celery, parsley, and salt and pepper to taste. Sauté over medium heat, stirring with a wooden spoon, for about 2 minutes, or until the onion becomes slightly translucent.

2 Add the vegetable stock, increase the heat to medium-high, and bring to a full boil. Cook uncovered for 15 minutes, stirring occasionally.

3 Crack an egg into a small bowl and gently add to the hot stock, making sure the yolk does not break. Repeat for the remaining eggs, adding them one at a time. Spoon some of the stock on top of the eggs and cook for about 2 minutes, or until the egg whites have firmed up.

4 Place a slice of toasted bread in each of four bowls. Ladle the soup into the bowls and carefully top each with an egg. Serve hot.

VARIATION: You can bulk up this soup by adding some quick-cooking vegetables, such as spinach or zucchini, when you add the stock.

MAMMA'S CLASSIC PASTINA

◇◇◇◇◇◇◇◇◇◇◇◇◇◇◇◇◇◇◇ PASTINA DI MAMMA ◇◇◇◇◇◇◇◇◇◇◇◇◇◇◇◇◇◇◇

Italian penicillin—that's what a bowl of pastina is! The word "pastina" refers to the small size of the pasta used in this soup, but it also refers to the countless versions of the soup itself. Moms and dads all over Italy prepare this for their youngsters in the winter months. Italians wholeheartedly believe that any child suffering from a cold, fever, or flu will be made better by a bowl of pastina. The cubed chicken adds protein to this dish.

SERVES 4
PREP TIME: 5 minutes
COOK TIME: 25 minutes

2 quarts water

1 carrot, finely diced

½ celery stalk, finely diced

½ small onion, diced

1 tablespoon chopped
fresh parley

1 pound chicken
breast tenders, cut
into ½-inch cubes

1 tablespoon olive oil

½ large vegetable or
chicken bouillon cube

½ cup orzo pasta

Sea salt

Grated Parmigiano-Reggiano
cheese (optional)

1 In a 3-quart soup pot, combine the water, carrot, celery, onion, parsley, chicken, olive oil, and bouillon cube and bring to a boil over high heat. Cook, stirring occasionally, for 15 minutes, or until the vegetables are tender.

2 Add the orzo and cook according to the package directions (usually 8 to 10 minutes), stirring occasionally. Season with salt.

3 Spoon into bowls. If desired, garnish with Parmigiano.

PAIRING TIP: While cheeses are often served as an antipasto, it's not uncommon in Italy to also serve some dry cheese after a meal—especially a light meal, like a soup or salad. Serve some chunks of Parmigiano-Reggiano or Pecorino Romano after a bowl of this classic pastina to round out the dinner.

IMPERIAL SOUP

◇◇◇◇◇◇◇◇◇◇◇◇◇◇◇◇◇ ZUPPA IMPERIALE ◇◇◇◇◇◇◇◇◇◇◇◇◇◇◇◇◇

Emilia-Romagna, Abruzzo, Le Marche—all these regions claim *zuppa imperiale* is a classic of their locality. But is it a soup or a frittata? While the recipe varies from region to region, this dish is always unique, satisfying, and hearty. Our version uses canned stock, but in Italy they often make their own from scratch.

SERVES 4
PREP TIME: 10 minutes
COOK TIME: 20 minutes

4 large eggs, separated

3 tablespoons
all-purpose flour

½ cup grated
Parmigiano-Reggiano cheese,
plus more for topping

1 tablespoon chopped
fresh parsley

¼ teaspoon grated nutmeg

Sea salt

Freshly ground black pepper

8 cups chicken, vegetable,
or beef stock

1 Preheat the oven to 350°F. Line a baking sheet with parchment paper.

2 In a medium bowl, whisk together the egg yolks, flour, Parmigiano, parsley, nutmeg, and salt and pepper to taste.

3 In a separate medium bowl, with an electric mixer, beat the egg whites for about 2 minutes, or until stiff peaks form. Using a rubber spatula, fold the whites into the egg yolks, using a gentle hand so as not to deflate the beaten whites.

4 Spread the mixture onto the baking sheet and bake for 15 minutes.

5 Meanwhile, in a large soup pot, bring the stock to a boil over high heat and boil for 3 to 4 minutes, until the stock is very hot.

6 Remove the eggs from the oven and cut them into crouton-size cubes.

7 Divide the hot stock among four bowls and add the egg cubes on top. Top with additional Parmigiano.

SHORTCUT: To save you time at dinnertime, you can prep and bake the eggs in the morning and refrigerate them until they're ready to be added to the hot stock.

PANZANELLA

◇◇◇◇◇◇◇◇◇◇◇◇◇◇◇◇◇◇◇ INSALATA PANZANELLA ◇◇◇◇◇◇◇◇◇◇◇◇◇◇◇◇◇◇◇

A classic Tuscan recipe, this salad is the perfect summer lunch or dinner, when tomatoes are at their peak. Light, refreshing, and genuine, it was once considered poor man's food because it used day-old bread. This is essentially the salad version of Tuscan Bread and Tomato Soup (page 23).

SERVES 4
PREP TIME: 10 minutes
COOK TIME: 10 minutes

4 medium-thick slices day-old Italian bread, cubed

6 tablespoons extra-virgin olive oil, divided

¼ cup red wine vinegar

4 medium tomatoes

1 small red onion, chopped

3 tablespoons chopped fresh basil

½ cup pitted and halved black olives

Sea salt

Freshly ground black pepper

1 Preheat the oven to 400°F.

2 Using tongs, toss the bread and 3 tablespoons of olive oil on a baking sheet and toast for 10 minutes.

3 Meanwhile, in a small bowl, whisk together the remaining 3 tablespoons of olive oil and the vinegar. Set aside.

4 Cut the tomatoes into ½-inch dice and place them in a large salad bowl. Add the onion, basil, and olives. Season with salt and pepper. Toss to fully combine. Add the oil and vinegar dressing and toss.

5 Remove the bread from the oven and mix it into the salad. Serve immediately or let stand for up to 30 minutes.

VARIATION: This is the standard recipe for an authentic panzanella, but to add some additional fuel or modify it to your taste, you can include mozzarella cheese, capers, anchovies, and cucumbers—all welcome additions.

PESTO PASTA SALAD

×◇×◇×◇×◇×◇×◇×◇×◇×◇×◇ INSALATA DI PASTA CON PESTO ×◇×◇×◇×◇×◇×◇×◇×◇×◇×◇

Adored by all of Italy, young and old alike, basil pesto is a specialty of the region of Liguria. Basil, pine nuts, and freshly grated cheese are key ingredients in this simple but iconic summery dish. While most often served with pasta, this no-cook sauce can also be used as a spread on panini or even to top some grilled meats. In Italy, the pesto is often prepared with a mortar and pestle, but using a food processor speeds things up and results in a smoother sauce.

SERVES 4
PREP TIME: 10 minutes
COOK TIME: 15 minutes

Sea salt

12 ounces fusilli pasta

4 to 5 cups fresh basil leaves

2 garlic cloves, peeled

3 tablespoons pine nuts

4 tablespoons extra-virgin olive oil, divided

¼ cup grated Parmigiano-Reggiano cheese

4 precooked sweet Italian sausages, each cut into 8 to 10 slices

1 pint cherry tomatoes, halved

1 In a 6-quart pot, bring 4 quarts of salted water to a boil over high heat. Add the fusilli and cook according to the package directions.

2 Meanwhile, in a food processor, combine the basil, garlic, pine nuts, and 3 tablespoons of olive oil and pulse for 1 minute, stopping to press down the basil leaves. Add the Parmigiano and pulse until a creamy paste is formed, about 1 minute. Set aside.

3 In a medium skillet, heat the remaining 1 tablespoon of oil over medium heat. Add sausage slices and heat for 1 minute.

4 Drain the pasta and add it to a large serving platter. Add the pesto, sausages, and tomatoes and mix until everything is combined. Serve immediately or at room temperature.

VARIATION: While basil is typically the key ingredient in a classic pesto, spinach or arugula can also be used to change things up a bit. And if you can't find pine nuts, almonds and walnuts make great substitutes.

CAPRESE-STYLE TORTELLINI SALAD

◇◇◇◇◇◇◇◇◇◇ INSALATA DI TORTELLINI IN STILE CAPRESE ◇◇◇◇◇◇◇◇◇◇

Caprese salad is a classic summery salad from the island of Capri, off the Amalfi Coast. It is believed that a war veteran wanted to create a dish that represented the colors of the Italian flag, so he selected a handful of ingredients that contained red, white, and green. I've added tortellini to the classic recipe, which turns this light salad into a full meal.

SERVES 4 to 6
PREP TIME: 10 minutes
COOK TIME: 10 minutes

Sea salt

1 (20-ounce) package fresh cheese tortellini

3 tomatoes, cut into 1-inch cubes

1 pound ciliegine (cherry-size) mozzarella balls, drained, or 1 pound mozzarella cheese, cubed

1 cup fresh basil leaves

3 tablespoons extra-virgin olive oil

1 teaspoon dried oregano

1 Bring a large pot of salted water to a boil over high heat. Add the tortellini and cook according to the package directions. Pay close attention to the timing, as they can easily overcook.

2 Meanwhile, place the tomatoes on a large serving platter, season with salt, and mix. Add the mozzarella, basil, oil, and oregano and toss to combine.

3 Drain the tortellini and add them to the platter. Mix gently to avoid breaking the tortellini. Serve hot or at room temperature.

PAIRING TIP: A dry white wine, such as Pinot Grigio, will pair nicely with both the mozzarella and tomatoes in this dish, as it's light and fruity and does not compete with the acid of the tomatoes.

ANTIPASTO SALAD

◇◇◇◇◇◇◇◇◇◇◇◇◇◇◇◇◇◇◇◇ INSALATA ANTIPASTO ◇◇◇◇◇◇◇◇◇◇◇◇◇◇◇◇◇◇◇◇

nsalata antipasto takes many of the ingredients typically found on an antipasto platter and turns them into a delicious salad. None of the items in this dish require cooking, so your time will be mostly spent cutting the ingredients. This salad is delicious and satisfying as is, but be sure to have some delicious crusty bread handy because it will serve nicely to mop up all the lovely dressing! There's no specific recipe for this salad, and all the ingredients are simply suggestions. This version uses baby spinach because it saves on cutting and rinsing time.

SERVES 6
PREP TIME: 20 minutes

FOR THE DRESSING

¼ cup extra-virgin olive oil

Juice of ½ lemon

1 teaspoon dried oregano

½ teaspoon sea salt

Freshly ground black pepper

FOR THE SALAD

4 cups baby spinach

2 (5-ounce) cans Italian tuna packed in oil, undrained

1 (12-ounce) jar giardiniera (pickled mixed vegetables), drained, rinsed, and chopped

1 (8-ounce) container ciliegine (cherry-size) mozzarella balls, drained

1 (12-ounce) jar roasted red peppers, rinsed under cold water and cut into ¼-inch-wide strips

5 ounces sliced prosciutto, cut into strips

½ cup pitted and halved Italian black or green olives

½ medium red onion, chopped

1 pint cherry tomatoes, halved

1 **TO MAKE THE DRESSING:** In a small bowl, whisk together the olive oil, lemon juice, oregano, salt, and pepper to taste.

2 **TO MAKE THE SALAD:** In a large salad bowl, toss together the spinach and dressing. Flake in the tuna, add the oil from the cans, and toss to combine.

3 Add the giardiniera, mozzarella balls, roasted peppers, prosciutto, olives, onion, and cherry tomatoes and toss well until everything is fully incorporated.

4 Serve immediately or let stand for no more than 30 minutes.

INGREDIENT TIP: Giardiniera is a blend of vegetables packed in a white vinegar brine. The mixture usually contains sliced carrots, cauliflower, celery, cherry peppers, and sometimes a few green olives. Ciliegine are cherry-size balls of fresh mozzarella (*ciliegie* means "cherries") that come packaged in water or brine.

ITALIAN RICE SALAD

INSALATA DI RISO

Ideal for picnics, days at the beach, and even lunch boxes, an Italian rice salad is a staple dish served all over Italy, with many variations. You can serve it immediately, while it's still warm, which is my favorite way, or you can let it come to room temperature or even chill it. Rice soaks up a lot of oil, which makes this dish that much more delicious.

SERVES 4 to 6
PREP TIME: 10 minutes
COOK TIME: 20 minutes

Sea salt

1½ cups Arborio rice

¼ cup extra-virgin olive oil, plus more to taste

2 (5-ounce) cans Italian tuna packed in oil, undrained

4 large hard-boiled eggs, peeled and diced

¾ cup finely cubed deli-style ham

¼ pound deli-style salami or soppressata, cubed

½ cup shredded mozzarella cheese

½ cup grated Parmigiano-Reggiano cheese

1 Bring a large pot of salted water to a boil over high heat. Add the rice and cook until tender, 18 to 20 minutes. Drain well.

2 Meanwhile, chop and prepare the rest of the ingredients.

3 In a large serving bowl, combine the drained rice and olive oil. Flake in the tuna, add the oil from the tuna cans, and mix well to coat the rice with the oils.

4 Add the eggs, ham, salami, mozzarella, and Parmigiano and mix well. Add more oil, if desired, as the rice tends to soak it up. Season with salt and serve hot or at room temperature.

VARIATION: Although this recipe is very filling, you can add olives, canned corn, or pickled vegetables. You can use long-grain rice, as well; the final result will be just a bit less creamy.

CHEESY POLENTA WITH SAUTÉED GREENS, PAGE 57

CHAPTER 3

PASTA, RISOTTO, AND POLENTA

Ravioli in Butter and Sage Sauce | *Ravioli in Burro e Salvia* 39

Ravioli with Tomato-Basil Sauce |
Ravioli con Salsa di Pomodori e Basilico 40

Tortellini in Broth | *Tortellini in Brodo* 41

Creamy Gnocchi with Gorgonzola and Walnuts |
Gnocchi Cremosi con Gorgonzola e Noci 42

Penne with Ham and Peas in Cream Sauce |
Penne, Panna e Prosciutto 44

Calabrian-Style Penne | *Penne alla Calabrese* 45

Mostaccioli in Pink Sauce | *Mostaccioli in Salsa Rosa* 46

Cavatelli with Broccoli Pesto | *Cavatelli con Pesto di Broccoli* 47

Rigatoni with Vegetarian Ragù | *Rigatoni
con Ragù Vegetariano* 48

Spaghetti Puttanesca 49

Spaghetti in Clam Sauce | *Spaghetti alle Vongole* 50

Quick Meat Sauce with Fettuccine |
Fettuccine con Ragù Veloce di Carne 51

continued

Mushroom Risotto | *Risotto con Funghi* 52

Risotto Milanese | *Risotto alla Milanese* 53

Risotto with Peas and Pancetta | *Risotto con Piselli e Pancetta* 54

Polenta with Sausage and Peppers |
Polenta con Salcicce e Peperoni 55

Polenta with Sautéed Mushrooms | *Polenta con Funghi Saltate* 56

Cheesy Polenta with Sautéed Greens |
Polenta con Verdure Saltate 57

RAVIOLI IN BUTTER AND SAGE SAUCE

◇◇◇◇◇◇◇◇◇◇◇◇◇◇◇◇◇ RAVIOLI IN BURRO E SALVIA ◇◇◇◇◇◇◇◇◇◇◇◇◇◇◇◇◇

Can a sauce really be so simple, economical, quick, and delicious as this one? It sure can! Ravioli tossed with butter and sage sauce is a classic combination that cooks in record time and is ideal for weeknight dinners, but it's also sophisticated enough for weekends or even for that dinner party you've been meaning to put together. In Italy many serve this dish with home-made ravioli, but using fresh or frozen ravioli from your grocery store will save substantial prep time. I find that the fresh ones, which you can find in the refrigerated aisle (or sometimes in the dairy section), are best. Choose a filling that is not too overpowering, such as ricotta cheese or pumpkin.

SERVES 4
PREP TIME: 5 minutes
COOK TIME: 15 minutes

Sea salt

1 pound fresh ravioli

8 tablespoons (1 stick) unsalted butter, cubed

3 garlic cloves, minced

¼ cup sage leaves, cut into ribbons

Freshly ground black pepper

¼ cup grated Parmigiano-Reggiano cheese

1 In a 6-quart pot, bring 4 quarts of salted water to a boil over high heat. Add the ravioli and cook, stirring occasionally, for 1 minute less than the package directions. Take care not to overcook them or they will open up.

2 Meanwhile, in a large sauté pan, melt the butter over low heat and cook for 2 to 3 minutes, until the butter is slightly browned but not burned. It will get foamy. Add the garlic and sage and mix well. Season with salt and pepper.

3 Drain the ravioli and add them to the pan. Mix gently to combine and cook them in the sauce for 1 minute.

4 Divide the ravioli among four serving plates, spoon some of the butter sauce on top, and top each serving with 1 tablespoon Parmigiano. Serve hot.

PAIRING TIP: Chopped toasted walnuts or pecans are a great addition to this dish. Top each serving with 1 tablespoon nuts just before serving.

RAVIOLI WITH TOMATO-BASIL SAUCE

◇◇◇◇◇◇◇◇◇ RAVIOLI CON SALSA DI POMODORI E BASILICO ◇◇◇◇◇◇◇◇◇

W idely used all over Italy, this traditional tomato-basil sauce comes together quickly, uses just a few basic ingredients, and is full of flavor. Although it's a classic dish, everyone still has their own version. Mine takes mere minutes to prepare and calls for very simple ingredients. By the time the water is boiling, the sauce is almost cooked. Here, we're pairing it up with ravioli, but you could use any dry or fresh pasta instead.

SERVES 4 to 6
PREP TIME: 5 minutes
COOK TIME: 20 minutes

Sea salt

2 tablespoons olive oil

½ small yellow or white onion, finely diced

2 garlic cloves, finely minced

1 (28-ounce) can crushed tomatoes

1 cup water

2 tablespoons chopped fresh basil, plus basil leaves for garnish

1 (20-ounce) package fresh or frozen cheese ravioli

Grated Parmigiano-Reggiano or Pecorino Romano cheese (optional)

1 In a 6-quart pot, bring 4 quarts of salted water to a boil over high heat.

2 Meanwhile, in a medium saucepan, heat the oil over medium heat. Add the onion and sauté for 2 to 3 minutes until it's almost translucent. Add the garlic and cook for 1 minute longer, or until golden. Carefully add the tomatoes; they will splatter as they hit the hot oil. Add the water, season with salt, then stir in the basil. Reduce the heat to low, cover, and let the sauce simmer for 15 minutes to thicken.

3 Add the ravioli to the boiling water, stir, and cook according to the package directions. Do not overcook or they will burst open. Drain the ravioli and return them to the pot they cooked in. Add about 1 cup of the cooked tomato sauce and gently mix.

4 Divide the ravioli among serving plates. Top each dish with about ¼ cup of additional sauce and garnish with a basil leaf. If desired, sprinkle with grated cheese. Serve hot.

INGREDIENT TIP: Fresh or frozen prepared ravioli are a wonderful weeknight dinner option. They cook even faster than dried pasta, and are more filling. Read the cooking directions carefully, as they can easily overcook.

TORTELLINI IN BROTH

TORTELLINI IN BRODO

Tortellini in brodo is a classic dish served in northern Italy, especially in the city of Bologna in the Emilia-Romagna region, which is where this dish is believed to have originated. Tortellini are often served in a simple broth and topped with freshly grated Parmesan cheese—another specialty of this region. Both the stock and the tortellini are often made from scratch in Bologna, which turns this into a very labor-intensive meal. This streamlined version cuts that time to 30 minutes.

SERVES 4
PREP TIME: 10 minutes
COOK TIME: 20 minutes

2 tablespoons olive oil

1 yellow or white onion, diced

1 celery stalk, finely diced

2 carrots, finely diced

2 tablespoons chopped fresh parsley

2 tablespoons canned crushed tomatoes

10 cups water

1 large vegetable bouillon cube

Sea salt

Freshly ground black pepper

1 pound fresh tortellini (cheese or spinach)

2 cups baby spinach

Grated Parmigiano-Reggiano cheese (optional)

1 In a large soup pot, heat the oil over medium heat for 1 minute. Add the onion, celery, carrots, parsley, and tomatoes and simmer for 1 to 2 minutes, until the vegetables have slightly softened.

2 Increase the heat to high, add the water and bouillon cube, season with salt and pepper, and bring to a full boil. Boil for 10 minutes.

3 Add the tortellini and cook according to the package directions. Take care not to overcook or they will burst open. During the last 2 minutes of cooking time, add the spinach and stir to wilt. Remove from the heat and serve immediately. If desired, top with Parmigiano.

INGREDIENT TIP: Refrigerated tortellini and ravioli are a wonderful dinner choice when you're pressed for time. But pay close attention to the cooking time. In fact, it would be wise to taste one of the tortellini or ravioli 1 to 2 minutes before the cooking time listed on the package; I sometimes find the listed time is 1 to 2 minutes longer than it should be. Overcooking the stuffed pastas will result in burst tortellini and ravioli, with the filling escaping out.

CREAMY GNOCCHI WITH GORGONZOLA AND WALNUTS

◇◇◇◇◇◇◇◇◇ GNOCCHI CREMOSI CON GORGONZOLA E NOCI ◇◇◇◇◇◇◇◇◇

Gnocchi are little potato dumplings that originate from northern Italy, where the colder climate is ideal for growing potatoes. They are wonderful and light. And unlike pasta, which takes about 10 minutes to cook to perfection, gnocchi cook in just a few minutes, making them the ideal option for super quick dinners. They are adaptable and work in many recipes that call for pasta. Many traditional recipes begin by making the gnocchi from scratch, but buying them prepared cuts out a lot of time and prep work.

SERVES 4
PREP TIME: 5 minutes
COOK TIME: 15 minutes

Sea salt

¾ cup chopped walnuts, divided

½ cup whole milk

4 ounces Gorgonzola cheese, crumbled

1 pound store-bought potato gnocchi

1 In a 6-quart pot, bring 4 quarts of salted water to a boil over high heat.

2 Meanwhile, in a large sauté pan, toast the walnuts over medium heat for 1 to 2 minutes, stirring often and paying close attention so they do not burn or they will turn bitter. Remove from the pan.

3 In the same pan used to toast the nuts, bring the milk to a light boil over medium heat. When bubbles are forming at the edges of the pan, remove from the heat and add the Gorgonzola. Stir until the cheese is melted and the mixture is creamy. Add ½ cup of the toasted walnuts and stir to combine.

4 Add the gnocchi to the boiling water and cook according to the package directions (usually 2 to 3 minutes). They are cooked when they float to the top.

5 Drain the gnocchi and add them to the pan with the cream sauce. Stir to combine.

6 Transfer to plates and sprinkle the remaining ¼ cup walnuts on top.

INGREDIENT TIP: Gorgonzola cheese comes in sharp or mild flavors, depending on its age. The younger cheese is sweeter with a milder taste, while the older variety is tangier. Choose according to your preference.

VARIATION: If you're looking for a much milder flavor, instead of Gorgonzola add 1 cup whole-milk ricotta cheese. Because ricotta is wetter than Gorgonzola, reduce the amount of milk to ¼ cup.

PENNE WITH HAM AND PEAS IN CREAM SAUCE

◇◇◇◇◇◇◇◇◇◇◇◇◇◇◇ PENNE, PANNA E PROSCIUTTO ◇◇◇◇◇◇◇◇◇◇◇◇◇◇◇

Penne, panna e prosciutto is a classic dish served throughout Italy. It's especially prepared by busy parents who struggle to get their children to eat some vegetables. The combination of cream and Parmesan results in a super creamy and velvety sauce, while the ham offers a bit of saltiness. In Italy, it is often prepared with fresh peas, especially in springtime, but using frozen ones makes this the perfect dish any time of year.

SERVES 4 to 6
PREP TIME: 5 minutes
COOK TIME: 20 minutes

Sea salt

1 pound penne pasta

3 tablespoons olive oil

1 small yellow or white onion, chopped

1 (12-ounce) bag frozen peas

¼ cup water

½ pound deli-style ham, cubed or cut into strips

¾ cup heavy cream

¼ cup grated Parmigiano-Reggiano cheese

Freshly ground black pepper

VARIATION: The word *prosciutto* refers to both cooked and cured ham. While this dish is typically prepared with cooked ham, feel free to use the cured kind.

1 In a 6-quart pot, bring 4 quarts of salted water to a boil over high heat. Add the penne and cook for 1 to 2 minutes less than the package directions.

2 Meanwhile, in a large sauté pan, heat the oil and onion over medium heat and cook for about 2 minutes, or until the onion is slightly softened and translucent.

3 Add the peas and water and cook for 5 to 7 minutes, until the peas are slightly softened. Add the ham and cook for an additional 3 minutes, stirring occasionally. Add the cream and bring everything to a low simmer. Reduce the heat and cook the sauce and peas together for an additional 5 minutes to thicken the cream slightly.

4 Reserving about ½ cup of the pasta water, drain the pasta and add to the pan with the peas. Add the reserved pasta water, toss to combine, and cook for an additional 1 to 2 minutes, until the pasta is fully cooked.

5 Remove the pan from the heat and add the Parmigiano, mixing well to combine. Season with salt and pepper. Serve hot.

CALABRIAN-STYLE PENNE

PENNE ALLA CALABRESE

The food of Calabria is spicy, pungent, and minimalist. One of the most widely used ingredients in Calabria is chile peppers: fresh, dried, as a paste, or as pepper flakes. Along with other pungent ingredients—such as anchovies, capers, and olives—Calabrian chiles always seem to find a way into pasta dishes and sauces. This recipe is definitely spicy, so feel free to adjust the amount of heat according to your preference.

SERVES 4 to 6
PREP TIME: 5 minutes
COOK TIME: 25 minutes

Sea salt

1 pound penne or other tubular pasta

3 tablespoons olive oil

2 garlic cloves, minced

4 anchovy fillets packed in oil, drained

2 tablespoons Calabrian chile paste

1 (28-ounce) can crushed tomatoes

½ cup olives in brine, drained and chopped

2 tablespoons capers, rinsed

Freshly ground black pepper

Grated Pecorino Romano cheese (optional)

1 In a 6-quart pot, bring 4 quarts of salted water to a boil over high heat. Add the penne and cook 2 minutes less than the package directions.

2 Meanwhile, in a large sauté pan, heat the oil over medium heat. Add the garlic and anchovies and sauté for 2 minutes, breaking the anchovies up with a wooden spoon as they sauté. Add the chile paste and mix well into the other ingredients.

3 Add the tomatoes, olives, and capers and stir to incorporate. Season with salt and pepper and cook the sauce for 15 minutes.

4 Reserving about ¼ cup of the pasta water, drain the pasta and add to the pan with the sauce and mix to combine. Add the reserved pasta water and cook a minute or 2 to finish the pasta. Serve with grated Romano, if desired.

VARIATION: Italian Calabrian chile paste has become readily available at many grocery stores and markets, but if you cannot find it, you can substitute red pepper flakes and add them in step 4. The amount is up to you.

MOSTACCIOLI IN PINK SAUCE

◇◇◇◇◇◇◇◇◇◇◇◇◇◇◇◇◇ MOSTACCIOLI IN SALSA ROSA ◇◇◇◇◇◇◇◇◇◇◇◇◇◇◇◇◇

This dish from Rome brings together a classic red sauce and a simple white sauce (aka béchamel) because two sauces are better than one! Together, they create a creamy, delicate, and inventive pink sauce. It pairs perfectly with mostaccioli, a tube-style dried pasta. In Rome, this sauce is often made with cream, but I find using whole milk provides enough creaminess.

SERVES 4
PREP TIME: 10 minutes
COOK TIME: 20 minutes

Sea salt

1 pound mostaccioli or other tubular pasta

2 tablespoons olive oil

½ small onion, finely chopped

2 garlic cloves, minced

1½ cups canned crushed tomatoes

Freshly ground black pepper

3 tablespoons unsalted butter

3 tablespoons all-purpose flour

1½ cups whole milk

Grated Parmigiano-Reggiano or Pecorino Romano cheese (optional)

PAIRING TIP: The perfect starter for this dish is a light cheese antipasto of diced provolone, marinated ciliegine (cherry-size) mozzarella balls, and small chunks of Parmesan, served with grissini (breadsticks) or focaccia.

1 In a 6-quart pot, bring 4 quarts of salted water to a boil over high heat. Add the pasta, stir, and cook to about 1 minute less than the package directions.

2 Meanwhile, in a large sauté pan, heat the oil over medium heat. Add the onion and garlic and sauté for 1 minute, or until the onion is slightly softened and garlic is golden but not burned. Add the crushed tomatoes and season with salt and pepper. Stir everything to combine, reduce the heat to low, cover, and simmer for 10 minutes to thicken the sauce slightly.

3 While the pasta and red sauce cook, in a small saucepan, melt the butter over medium heat. Add the flour, season with salt and pepper, and whisk for about 2 minutes, or until smooth. Reduce the heat to low and slowly whisk in the milk. Increase the heat to medium-high and cook the white sauce for 2 to 3 minutes, until bubbling and thickened.

4 Add the white sauce to the red sauce and mix well. Drain the pasta and add it to the now pink sauce. Mix well to coat and cook the pasta for 1 minute.

5 Remove from the heat and stir in grated cheese, if desired.

CAVATELLI WITH BROCCOLI PESTO

◇◇◇◇◇◇◇◇◇◇◇ CAVATELLI CON PESTO DI BROCCOLI ◇◇◇◇◇◇◇◇◇◇◇

P asta and broccoli are a favorite dinner in southern Italy. This dish uses minimal ingredients, cooks quickly, and is also very economical. In this recipe, I've made a pesto out of the broccoli, rather than cooking it along with the pasta. I also left the traditional pine nuts out of the pesto, which results in a lighter-tasting final dish.

SERVES 4
PREP TIME: 10 minutes
COOK TIME: 15 minutes

Sea salt

12 ounces cavatelli pasta

4 cups broccoli florets

½ cup fresh basil leaves

¼ cup extra-virgin olive oil

2 garlic cloves, peeled

½ cup grated Parmigiano-Reggiano or Pecorino Romano cheese, or a combination of both

1 In a 6-quart pot, bring 4 quarts of salted water to a boil over high heat. Add the cavatelli and cook according to the package directions.

2 Meanwhile, in a medium saucepan, combine the broccoli florets and enough water to cover them. Bring to a full boil over high heat and cook for 5 minutes, or until the broccoli is just slightly tender.

3 Drain the broccoli and transfer to a food processor. Add the basil, oil, and garlic and pulse for several minutes, or until a creamy consistency forms. Scrape down the sides and add the cheese, then pulse again a few times until the mixture is well incorporated.

4 Reserving ¼ cup of the pasta water, drain the pasta and transfer to a large serving platter. Add the pesto and mix to combine. Add some of the pasta water, a few tablespoons at a time, to smooth out the pesto. Season with salt and serve hot or at room temperature.

VARIATION: For a more savory pesto, add a few oil-packed anchovy fillets to the food processor along with the garlic and oil.

RIGATONI WITH VEGETARIAN RAGÙ

◇◇◇◇◇◇◇◇◇◇ RIGATONI CON RAGÙ VEGETARIANO ◇◇◇◇◇◇◇◇◇◇

This vegetable ragù is a delicious pasta sauce that's simple, healthy, and hearty. It's a wonderful option for the vegetarians in your life (and vegans, if you leave out the cheese), but also very much enjoyed by those who eat meat. Because this is a thick sauce, I prefer using a sturdy tubular pasta, such as rigatoni, which stands up well to the thick sauce. *(Photograph on page vi.)*

SERVES 4 to 6
PREP TIME: 10 minutes
COOK TIME: 20 minutes

3 tablespoons olive oil

½ small onion, diced

1 small eggplant, diced

1 medium bell pepper, seeded and diced

2 small zucchini, diced

8 ounces small cremini mushrooms, halved

2 tablespoons chopped fresh parsley

1 (28-ounce) can crushed tomatoes

1 cup water

Sea salt

Freshly ground black pepper

12 ounces rigatoni pasta

Grated Parmesan or Pecorino Romano cheese

1 In a large sauté pan, heat the oil over medium heat for 1 minute. Add the onion, eggplant, bell pepper, zucchini, mushrooms, and parsley and sauté, stirring occasionally, for about 5 minutes, or until the vegetables have softened up and the onion is translucent.

2 Add the crushed tomatoes and water, season with salt and pepper, and simmer the sauce for 15 minutes, until it has thickened and the vegetables have further softened.

3 Meanwhile, in a 6-quart pot, bring 4 quarts of salted water to a boil over high heat. Add the rigatoni and cook for 2 minutes less than the package directions.

4 Drain the pasta and mix it into the sauté pan. Stir gently to coat the pasta with the sauce. Remove from the heat and serve topped with grated cheese.

VARIATION: Seek out a US-made Parmesan or Pecorino Romano cheese for this dish to make it vegetarian.

SPAGHETTI PUTTANESCA

A classic dish from Naples and the surrounding area, this sauce is quick, spicy, and full of flavor. Local olives are often used in Naples, but easier-to-find Kalamata olives are a great substitute. Add salt sparingly in this dish, because the capers, olives, and anchovies are all fairly salty ingredients. Spaghetti is recommended, but you could use any long, thin pasta of your choice.

SERVES 4 to 6
PREP TIME: 10 minutes
COOK TIME: 20 minutes

Sea salt

1 pound spaghetti

3 tablespoons olive oil

2 garlic cloves, minced

1 teaspoon red pepper flakes

3 tablespoons capers, rinsed

½ cup pitted Kalamata olives, halved

6 anchovies, chopped

2 cups canned crushed tomatoes

1 teaspoon dried oregano

1 In a 6-quart pot, bring 4 quarts of salted water to a boil over high heat. Add the spaghetti and cook for 2 minutes less than the package directions.

2 Meanwhile in a large sauté pan, heat the oil over medium heat. Add the garlic and pepper flakes and cook for 1 minute, or until the garlic is golden but not burned. Add the capers and olives and stir to combine. Add the anchovies and break them up with a wooden spoon. They will dissolve almost completely.

3 Add the crushed tomatoes and oregano. Season lightly with salt. Reduce the heat to medium-low and cook for 10 minutes to slightly thicken the sauce.

4 Reserving ¼ cup of the pasta water, drain the pasta. Add the pasta and a few tablespoons of the reserved pasta water to the sauce and mix to combine. Cook for an additional 2 minutes, mixing well to make sure the pasta is well coated with the sauce.

VARIATION: When fresh tomatoes are in season, skip the crushed tomatoes and use about 1 pound ripe tomatoes, finely diced, instead. Cook the sauce for an extra 5 minutes to concentrate the tomato flavor.

SPAGHETTI IN CLAM SAUCE

◇◇◇◇◇◇◇◇◇◇◇◇◇ SPAGHETTI ALLE VONGOLE ◇◇◇◇◇◇◇◇◇◇◇◇◇◇

This iconic dish, a classic seafood pasta of southern Italy, is usually served with a long, delicate pasta such as spaghetti or linguine. One variation is to add capers and olives, but I've left those out in this recipe to let the main ingredient, the clams, shine through. Red pepper flakes are a staple in southern Italy, but feel free to leave them out if you prefer a milder sauce that is just a bit more subtle.

SERVES 4 to 6
PREP TIME: 5 minutes
COOK TIME: 15 minutes

Sea salt

1 pound spaghetti or other long, thin pasta

3 pounds small clams, scrubbed clean

¼ cup olive oil

4 garlic cloves, minced

Red pepper flakes

1 cup dry white wine

1 tablespoon chopped fresh parsley

Freshly ground black pepper

1 In a 6-quart pot, bring 4 quarts of salted water to a boil over high heat. Add the spaghetti, stir, and cook to just under al dente, about 2 minutes less than the package directions.

2 Meanwhile, to prepare the clam sauce, close any of the open clams by giving them a quick tap, and discard any that don't close. In a large sauté pan, heat the oil over medium heat. Add the garlic and pepper flakes and stir for 1 minute. Add the clams and wine, cover, and cook for 6 to 7 minutes, until the clams have opened. Discard any clams that remain unopened after 7 minutes of cooking.

3 Drain the spaghetti and add to the pan with the clams. Add the parsley and mix to combine. Season with salt and pepper.

VARIATION: Want to mix things up a bit and serve this dish *rosso*? *Rosso* means "red" in Italian and it refers to simply adding some canned tomatoes to any dish. Add one 14.5-ounce can diced tomatoes to the pan before adding the clams and cook the tomatoes for about 5 minutes. Then add the clams and continue with the recipe as written. You will end up with a lovely red sauce that's a bit sturdier and heartier— and thus perfect for tubular pasta.

QUICK MEAT SAUCE WITH FETTUCCINE

FETTUCCINE CON RAGÙ VELOCE DI CARNE

A basic tomato sauce beefed up with ground meat is a dish served throughout Italy. While a typical meat sauce can take two or more hours to cook, using ground meat saves a lot of time. I suggest using lean beef, but you could use ground turkey or veal without adjusting the cooking time. Fresh fettuccine is great in this dish, but you could also use dried pasta.

SERVES 4
PREP TIME: 5 minutes
COOK TIME: 25 minutes

2 tablespoons olive oil

½ small yellow or white onion, finely diced

2 garlic cloves, minced

2 tablespoons chopped fresh basil

12 ounces ground beef (90% lean)

Sea salt

Freshly ground black pepper

1 (28-ounce) can crushed tomatoes

½ cup water

1 (12-ounce) package fresh fettuccine

Grated Parmigiano-Reggiano cheese (optional)

1 In a large sauté pan, heat the oil over medium heat for 1 minute. Add the onion, garlic, and basil and cook for 1 minute, or until the onion is slightly softened and the garlic is golden but not burned. Add the ground beef and use a wooden spoon to break the meat into bite-size chunks. Season with salt and pepper and brown the meat for 3 to 4 minutes, stirring often to prevent burning and sticking.

2 Stir in the crushed tomatoes and water, reduce the heat to medium-low, cover, and cook, stirring occasionally, for 20 minutes, or until the sauce has thickened.

3 Meanwhile, in a 6-quart pot, bring 4 quarts of salted water to a boil over high heat.

4 During the last 2 minutes of the sauce's cooking time, add the fettuccine to the boiling water and cook according to the package directions (usually only 2 to 3 minutes).

5 Drain the fettuccine, add it to the sauce, and stir. Serve hot topped with Parmigiano, if desired.

INGREDIENT TIP: I find lean ground beef at a ratio of 90/10 works best in this dish, as anything higher than 10% fat is a bit too fatty.

MUSHROOM RISOTTO

◇◇◇◇◇◇◇◇◇◇◇◇◇◇◇◇◇◇ RISOTTO CON FUNGHI ◇◇◇◇◇◇◇◇◇◇◇◇◇◇◇◇◇◇

R isotto is a specialty of northern Italy and is enjoyed in countless combinations, with mushrooms being a national favorite. But risotto in a 30-minute cookbook? Yes, it can be done! In fact, rice cooks perfectly in about 22 minutes. The only downside to risotto is that it requires constant stirring. But the process is calming and almost therapeutic.

SERVES 4 to 6
PREP TIME: 5 minutes
COOK TIME: 25 minutes

6 to 8 cups vegetable stock

¼ cup olive oil

½ medium yellow or white onion, diced

Sea salt

Freshly ground black pepper

1½ cups Arborio rice

½ cup dry white wine

8 ounces cremini or white button mushrooms, sliced

1 tablespoon unsalted butter

½ cup grated Parmigiano-Reggiano cheese

INGREDIENT TIP:
Arborio or Carnaroli rice should always be used when preparing risotto. One of the key attributes of any risotto is its creaminess, which can be achieved only by using a rice that is high in starch, such as Arborio or Carnaroli.

1 In a large soup pot, bring the stock to a boil. Reduce the heat to low, just to keep the stock warm as you prepare the risotto.

2 Meanwhile, in a large sauté pan, heat the oil over medium heat. Add the onion, season with salt and pepper, and stir to combine. Cook the onion for about 1 minute, until slightly softened. Add the rice and cook in the oil and onion, stirring for 1 minute, or until the rice turns slightly paler. Stir in the wine. Let the rice absorb the wine, which will take about 1 minute.

3 When the rice has absorbed the wine, add 2 ladles of the warm stock to the rice. Stir to combine and continue stirring until the liquid is absorbed. When the liquid is absorbed, add 2 more ladles of stock and stir again to combine. Continue the process of adding 2 ladles at a time of stock for about 17 minutes, at which point the rice will still be a few minutes underdone.

4 Add the mushrooms, stir well, and cook the mushrooms and rice together, stirring, for about 3 minutes.

5 Remove from the heat, stir in the butter and Parmigiano, and serve immediately.

RISOTTO MILANESE

◇◇◇◇◇◇◇◇◇◇◇◇◇◇◇◇◇◇◇◇◇◇ RISOTTO ALLA MILANESE ◇◇◇◇◇◇◇◇◇◇◇◇◇◇◇◇◇◇◇◇◇◇

Risotto alla milanese is a classic dish hailing from the city of Milan, although now it is served all over Italy. In essence, it's a simple risotto with a hallmark orange-yellowish color and flavor that come from the addition of saffron. Occasionally, bone marrow is added, I've left that out in this recipe, as it's not an ingredient that's readily available or appealing to everyone.

SERVES 4 to 6
PREP TIME: 5 minutes
COOK TIME: 25 minutes

6 to 8 cups vegetable stock

Generous pinch of saffron strands

¼ cup olive oil

½ medium yellow or white onion, diced

Sea salt

Freshly ground black pepper

1½ cups Arborio rice

½ cup dry white wine

1 tablespoon unsalted butter

½ cup grated Parmigiano-Reggiano cheese

1 In a large soup pot, bring the stock to a boil over high heat. Add the saffron strands, then reduce the heat to low, just to keep the stock warm as you prepare the risotto.

2 Meanwhile, in a large sauté pan, heat the oil over medium heat. Add the onion, season with salt and pepper, and stir to combine. Cook the onion for about 1 minute, or until slightly softened. Stir in the rice and cook, stirring, for 1 minute, or until the rice turns slightly paler. Stir in the wine. Let the rice absorb the wine, which will take about 1 minute.

3 When the rice has absorbed the wine, add 2 ladles of the warm stock to the rice. Stir to combine and continue stirring until the liquid is absorbed. When the liquid is absorbed, add 2 more ladles of stock and stir again to combine. Continue the process of adding 2 ladles at a time of stock, until the rice is almost cooked but still al dente, which will take about 20 minutes.

4 Remove from the heat, stir in the butter and Parmigiano, and serve immediately.

INGREDIENT TIP: One key component of any risotto is warm broth or stock. It's important that the stock be warm so the rice keeps cooking. Adding cold stock would stop the rice from cooking, which would add cooking time and result in a gummier risotto.

RISOTTO WITH PEAS AND PANCETTA

◇◇◇◇◇◇◇◇◇◇◇◇◇◇ RISOTTO CON PISELLI E PANCETTA ◇◇◇◇◇◇◇◇◇◇◇◇◇◇

Peas with pancetta is a classic combination for a side dish adored throughout all of Italy. Everyone seems to have their own preference when it comes to doneness for the peas. Some folks cook them for just a few minutes, while others cook them as long as 20 minutes. Depending on your preference, you can add them at the beginning of the cooking process, in the middle (as suggested in the recipe), or during the last 3 to 4 minutes of the risotto cooking time.

SERVES 4 to 6
PREP TIME: 5 minutes
COOK TIME: 25 minutes

6 to 8 cups vegetable stock

2 tablespoons olive oil

½ medium yellow or white onion, diced

4 ounces pancetta, diced

Sea salt

Freshly ground black pepper

1½ cups Arborio rice

½ cup dry white wine

1½ cups frozen peas

1 tablespoon unsalted butter

½ cup grated Parmigiano-Reggiano cheese

PAIRING TIP: A dry, crisp Pinot Grigio would not only be perfect to drink with this risotto, but would also be the ideal wine to use in cooking it.

1 In a large soup pot, bring the stock to a boil over high heat, then reduce the heat to low, just to keep it warm as you prepare the risotto.

2 In a large sauté pan, heat the oil over medium heat. Add the onion and pancetta, season with salt and pepper, and stir to combine. Cook for about 1 minute, or until the onion and pancetta are slightly softened. Stir in the rice and cook for 1 minute, until the rice turns slightly paler. Stir in the wine. Let the rice absorb the wine, which will take about 1 minute.

3 When the rice has absorbed the wine, add 2 ladles of the warm stock to the rice. Stir to combine and continue stirring until the liquid is absorbed. When the liquid is absorbed, add 2 more ladles of stock and stir again to combine. Continue the process of adding 2 ladles at a time of stock for about 10 minutes, at which point the rice will still be undercooked.

4 Add the peas and stir well, cooking the peas and rice together for the last 10 minutes, stirring during the process, and adding ladles of stock as needed.

5 Remove from the heat, stir in the butter and Parmigiano, and serve immediately.

POLENTA WITH SAUSAGE AND PEPPERS

◇◇◇◇◇◇◇◇◇◇◇◇◇ POLENTA CON SALCICCE E PEPERONI ◇◇◇◇◇◇◇◇◇◇◇◇◇

A naturally gluten-free specialty from northern Italy, polenta is the perfect dinner when you want a change from pasta or rice. A frequent accompaniment to polenta are sausages and peppers. The use of instant polenta and precooked sausages cuts cooking time substantially. I've given a range for the stock to use here because the exact amount will depend on your preferred style of enjoying polenta: The smaller amount of stock produces a thicker, stiffer polenta; the larger amount will result in a much creamier, smoother polenta.

SERVES 4 to 6
PREP TIME: 10 minutes
COOK TIME: 20 minutes

¼ cup olive oil

2 large red bell peppers, cut into 1-inch pieces

1 medium onion, diced

1 tablespoon chopped fresh parsley

Sea salt

Freshly ground black pepper

4 precooked sweet or hot Italian sausages, chopped

1 cup canned crushed tomatoes

½ cup water

4 to 6 cups chicken or vegetable stock

1½ cups instant polenta

1 tablespoon unsalted butter

1 In a large skillet, heat the oil over medium-high heat. Add the bell peppers, onion, parsley, and salt and black pepper to taste and stir to combine. Cook for 1 to 2 minutes, until the onions and peppers are slightly charred.

2 Stir in the sausage, crushed tomatoes, and water. Reduce the heat to medium-low and cook for 15 minutes, stirring occasionally to ensure nothing sticks to the pan. Add an additional tablespoon of oil or a few tablespoons of the stock if the mixture seems dry. The peppers will soften as they cook.

3 Meanwhile, in a large saucepan, bring the stock to a boil over high heat. Gradually add the polenta to the boiling stock and cook according to the package directions (usually 3 to 4 minutes), stirring constantly to prevent sticking.

4 Remove from the heat and add the butter. Spoon the polenta onto a large serving platter, then spoon the sausages and peppers on top. Serve family style.

POLENTA WITH SAUTÉED MUSHROOMS

POLENTA CON FUNGHI SALTATE

Another classic combination from northern Italy, especially the Piedmont region, is mushrooms and polenta. Perfect for the fall and winter months, mushrooms cook extremely quickly. They do require gentle cleaning, though, so use a damp paper towel to remove any noticeable dirt. Brown-skinned mushrooms such as cremini, porcini, and portobello all work wonderfully in this recipe. This recipe also works well with oven-roasted mushrooms. Follow the recipe as written, but instead of cooking the mushrooms on the stovetop, place them on a baking sheet and cook for 10 minutes at 375°F.

SERVES 4 to 6
PREP TIME: 10 minutes
COOK TIME: 15 minutes

4 to 6 cups vegetable stock

3 tablespoons olive oil

1½ pounds mixed brown-skinned mushrooms, cut into ½-inch-thick slices

1 tablespoon fresh thyme

2 garlic cloves, minced

Sea salt

Freshly ground black pepper

1½ cups instant polenta

2 tablespoons unsalted butter

¼ cup grated Parmigiano-Reggiano cheese

1. In a medium soup pot, bring the stock to a boil over high heat.

2. Meanwhile, in a large skillet, heat the oil over medium-low heat. Add the mushrooms, thyme, and garlic and stir to combine. Season with salt and pepper, stir, and cook the mushrooms for 10 minutes, or until they are a good deal softer and have released most of their natural liquid.

3. Gradually add the polenta to the boiling stock and cook according to the package directions (usually 3 to 4 minutes), stirring constantly to prevent sticking. Remove from the heat and stir in the butter and Parmigiano.

4. Spoon the polenta onto a large serving platter, then spoon the mushrooms on top. Serve family style.

PAIRING TIP: Make this dish vegetarian by choosing a US-made Parmesan (no animal rennet) and serve it with a vegetarian antipasto plate: Prepare a platter of olives, grilled red peppers cut into strips, pickled vegetables, and mushrooms marinated in brine. Jarred artichoke hearts would also work well.

CHEESY POLENTA WITH SAUTÉED GREENS

◇◇◇◇◇◇◇◇◇◇◇◇◇◇ POLENTA CON VERDURE SALTATE ◇◇◇◇◇◇◇◇◇◇◇◇◇◇

Hearty, quick, and nutritious, this dish is an alternative to serving polenta with the traditional mushrooms or sausage. Instead, it is topped with sautéed greens simply cooked with some olive oil and garlic. Packed with nutrients, this warm and comforting peasant dish comes together in 20 minutes.

SERVES 4 to 6
PREP TIME: 5 minutes
COOK TIME: 15 minutes

4 to 6 cups vegetable stock

¼ cup olive oil

2 garlic cloves, minced

1 bunch Swiss chard, cut into 1-inch pieces

Sea salt

Freshly ground black pepper

1½ cups instant polenta

1 tablespoon unsalted butter

½ cup grated Parmigiano-Reggiano cheese

½ cup shredded Fontina cheese

2 (10-ounce) bags baby spinach

1 In a medium soup pot, bring the stock to a boil over high heat.

2 Meanwhile, in a large skillet or sauté pan, heat the oil over medium-low heat. Add the garlic and cook for 1 minute, or until slightly golden but not burned. Add the chard, season with salt and pepper, and cook for 5 minutes, or until slightly wilted and softened. Add 1 to 2 tablespoons of stock from the soup pot if the pan is drying out too quickly.

3 Gradually add the polenta to the boiling stock and cook according to the package directions (usually 3 to 4 minutes), stirring constantly to prevent sticking. Remove the polenta from the heat and stir in the butter, Parmigiano, and Fontina.

4 Add the spinach to the vegetable pan and use tongs or a wooden spoon to pack the spinach down. It will wilt and cook in 1 to 2 minutes.

5 Spoon the polenta onto a large serving platter, then spoon the greens on top. Serve family style.

VARIATION: Spinach and Swiss chard cook quickly, but if you wanted to add sturdier vegetables, broccoli rabe and kale also work wonderfully. Add about 5 minutes of cooking time when sautéing the vegetables.

ORECCHIETTE WITH BROCCOLI RABE, PAGE 73

CHAPTER 4

VEGETARIAN SIDES AND MAINS

Genovese-Style Spinach | *Spinaci Genovese* 60

Leccese-Style Sweet Peppers | *Peperoni Leccese* 61

Scapece-Style Zucchini | *Zucchini alla Scapece* 62

Green Beans and Potato Mash | *Fagioli Verdi con Patate* 63

Stuffed Mushroom Caps | *Funghi Ripieni* 64

Oven-Roasted Stuffed Tomatoes | *Pomodori Ripieni al Forno* 65

Eggplant Pizzas | *Pizzette di Melanzane* 66

Vegetable Kebabs | *Spiedini di Verdure* 67

Eggs in Purgatory | *Uova in Purgatorio* 68

Three-Cheese Frittata | *Frittata Tre Formaggi* 69

Spinach and Mozzarella Frittata |
Frittata con Spinaci e Mozzarella 70

Pasta alla Norma 72

Orecchiette with Broccoli Rabe |
Orecchiette con le Cime di Rapa 73

Ziti with Cremini Mushrooms | *Ziti con Funghi Cremini* 74

GENOVESE-STYLE SPINACH

◇◇◇◇◇◇◇◇◇◇◇◇◇◇◇◇◇◇◇◇ SPINACI GENOVESE ◇◇◇◇◇◇◇◇◇◇◇◇◇◇◇◇◇◇◇◇

A dish typical of Genovese cuisine, this *contorno* (side dish) is simple, nutritious, and extremely quick. Spinach cooks in mere minutes, making it a great go-to vegetable during the week. Pine nuts and raisins add substance and offer a unique crunchy bite to this healthy dish.

SERVES 4
PREP TIME: 5 minutes
COOK TIME: 10 minutes

½ cup raisins

2 (12-ounce) bags
baby spinach

2 tablespoons olive oil

1 tablespoon chopped
fresh parsley

¼ cup pine nuts

Sea salt

Freshly ground black pepper

1 In a small bowl or cup, put the raisins in a cup of warm water and let stand for 10 minutes. Drain.

2 Meanwhile, put all the spinach in a sauté pan without adding water or oil. Cook the spinach over medium-low heat until it's wilted, about 3 minutes. Remove from the pan and set aside.

3 In the same pan, heat the oil over medium heat for 1 minute. Add the spinach and parsley and mix well to flavor the spinach with the oil. Add the raisins, pine nuts, and salt and pepper to taste and cook for 1 to 2 minutes, until everything is well seasoned.

VARIATION: Want to add some protein? Add a few chopped anchovies to the oil before you add the spinach. Cook them down for a minute or two, then add the spinach and continue with the recipe as written.

LECCESE-STYLE SWEET PEPPERS

◇◇◇◇◇◇◇◇◇◇◇◇◇◇◇◇◇◇◇◇◇◇ PEPERONI LECCESE ◇◇◇◇◇◇◇◇◇◇◇◇◇◇◇◇◇◇◇◇◇◇◇

This quick recipe, a specialty of Puglia, uses sweet bell peppers, which grow readily in southern Italy. Thanks in part to the dry soil, peppers of all colors are grown all over the region and used in countless recipes as sides or main courses. You can feel free to use a mixture of peppers, or stick with just one color. My personal preference is red peppers, as they are sweeter and more tender and cook a few minutes faster than their tougher green counterparts.

SERVES 4
PREP TIME: 10 minutes
COOK TIME: 20 minutes

½ cup fine breadcrumbs
(preferably from a bakery)

2 tablespoons capers, rinsed

1 tablespoon chopped
fresh parsley

¼ cup olive oil

4 large bell peppers (any
color), cut into ¼-inch dice

3 garlic cloves, minced

Sea salt

Freshly ground black pepper

½ cup water

1 In a small bowl, combine the breadcrumbs, capers, and parsley using a fork or your fingers. Set aside.

2 In a large sauté pan or skillet, heat the oil over medium heat. Add the bell peppers and sauté for 2 to 3 minutes, until they're slightly softened, stirring to make sure they do not stick to the pan. Add the garlic and season with salt and pepper. Add the water and sauté the peppers for 10 to 13 minutes, until they're softened and tender.

3 Reduce the heat to low, add the breadcrumb mixture, and stir to combine. Cook for 1 to 2 minutes, until the breadcrumbs have slightly toasted.

INGREDIENT TIP: When pan-fried, peppers soak up a good bit of olive oil, and you may have to add an additional tablespoon or two when you first sauté them. If the oil is disappearing too quickly, either reduce the heat or add a few additional tablespoons of water.

SCAPECE-STYLE ZUCCHINI

◇◇◇◇◇◇◇◇◇◇◇◇◇◇ ZUCCHINI ALLA SCAPECE ◇◇◇◇◇◇◇◇◇◇◇◇◇◇

This simple and delicious side dish is a specialty of the city of Naples. Zucchini is a beloved summer vegetable that's served in countless ways, from antipasto, to main courses, to the obvious side dishes, to meats or seafood. *Scapece* refers to cooking foods in vinegar. Although in this dish the popular zucchini takes center stage, Neapolitans are known for using the same method for all sorts of vegetables—and even meats.

SERVES 4
PREP TIME: 10 minutes
COOK TIME: 15 minutes

⅓ cup red or white
wine vinegar

¼ cup extra-virgin olive oil

2 tablespoons chopped
fresh mint leaves

2 garlic cloves, minced

Olive oil, for frying

3 to 4 medium zucchini,
cut into ¼-inch rounds

Sea salt

Freshly ground black pepper

1 In a small bowl, stir together the vinegar, extra-virgin olive oil, mint, and garlic and set aside.

2 Pour enough oil into a large sauté pan to come three-quarters of the way up. Heat the oil over high heat; it's hot enough to add the zucchini when it begins to bubble.

3 Line a large plate with paper towels. Working in batches (so as not to overcrowd the pan), fry the zucchini for 3 to 4 minutes, until they are crisp at the edges. Remove the zucchini from the oil and drain on the paper towels. Season with salt and pepper.

4 Transfer the zucchini to a serving bowl and add the vinegar dressing. Serve hot or at room temperature.

VARIATION: You can use the same exact method with eggplant. Just add 2 to 3 minutes to the cooking time.

GREEN BEANS AND POTATO MASH

◇◇◇◇◇◇◇◇◇◇◇◇◇◇◇◇◇◇ FAGIOLI VERDI CON PATATE ◇◇◇◇◇◇◇◇◇◇◇◇◇◇◇◇◇◇

A dish served frequently in southern Italy, especially Calabria, this humble recipe of green beans and potatoes is a staple of summer cuisine, when fresh green beans are at their peak. Using frozen Italian green beans substantially reduces the cooking time—not to mention that it makes it possible to enjoy this dish year round.

SERVES 4 to 6
PREP TIME: 10 minutes
COOK TIME: 10 minutes

Sea salt

2 to 3 medium potatoes, peeled and cubed

2 (16-ounce) bags frozen Italian green beans

3 tablespoons chopped fresh basil

3 garlic cloves, minced

3 tablespoons extra-virgin olive oil

Red pepper flakes (optional)

1 In a large soup pot, season about 2 quarts water with salt. Add the potatoes and green beans, bring to a boil over high heat, and cook for about 7 minutes, or until the green beans are fully cooked and the potatoes are fork-tender.

2 Drain the beans and potatoes and return them to the pot. With a wooden spoon or a potato masher, mash everything a number of times until the potatoes are broken down and resemble chunky mashed potatoes. The green beans should also be mashed slightly.

3 Add the basil, garlic, oil, and pepper flakes (if using) and mix everything to combine. Season with additional salt.

PAIRING TIP: This dish is often accompanied by some Italian cheeses to complete the meal. Some high-quality ricotta or mozzarella slices would be perfect.

INGREDIENT TIP: Italian green beans are wider and more tender than traditional green beans. Luckily for us, several popular brands have high-quality frozen Italian green beans. My go-to brands include Birds Eye, Wegman's, Kroger, and River Valley.

STUFFED MUSHROOM CAPS

◇◇◇◇◇◇◇◇◇◇◇◇◇◇◇◇◇◇◇◇◇◇ FUNGHI RIPIENI ◇◇◇◇◇◇◇◇◇◇◇◇◇◇◇◇◇◇◇◇◇◇◇◇◇◇

A perfect appetizer that's often served at Italian weddings, stuffed mushrooms also make the perfect vegetarian dinner, especially during the fall and winter months. While the ingredients for the stuffing vary from recipe to recipe, many southern Italians, not wanting to waste anything, often chop up and add the mushroom stems.

SERVES 4
PREP TIME: 10 minutes
COOK TIME: 20 minutes

8 large stuffing mushrooms

1 cup fine breadcrumbs (preferably from a bakery)

¼ cup walnuts, finely ground

3 tablespoons olive oil, plus more for drizzling

2 tablespoons chopped fresh parsley

2 to 3 garlic cloves, minced

Sea salt

Freshly ground black pepper

1 Preheat the oven to 375°F.

2 With a paring knife, take a very thin slice off the bottom of the mushroom stem and discard. With a damp paper towel, remove any visible dirt from the mushrooms. Carefully, so as not to break the mushroom cap, remove the stem from the cap and mince it finely. Add the minced stems to a medium bowl.

3 To the bowl with the minced stems, add the breadcrumbs, walnuts, oil, parsley, and garlic. Mix everything until the stuffing is moistened and well combined.

4 Arrange the mushroom caps on a baking sheet and season with salt and pepper. Using a tablespoon, generously stuff the caps with the filling, using the palm of your hand to pack it in. Lightly drizzle some additional oil on top. Bake for 18 to 20 minutes, until the tops are lightly browned.

INGREDIENT TIP: Mushroom stems are every bit as edible as the caps, and they make the perfect filling in this recipe. But if you'd prefer, you can mince the caps from an 8-ounce container of small button mushrooms. If desired, use a vegetarian cheese in place of the walnuts.

OVEN-ROASTED STUFFED TOMATOES

◇◇◇◇◇◇◇◇◇◇◇◇◇◇◇◇ POMODORI RIPIENI AL FORNO ◇◇◇◇◇◇◇◇◇◇◇◇◇◇◇◇

It seems every part of Italy has its own version of stuffed tomatoes. While Sicily stuffs tomatoes with lots of breadcrumbs, cheese, raisins, pine nuts, and anchovies, other areas use sausage meat, while still others use rice, which is an ever-popular choice in Rome. In this version, we're using the insides of the tomatoes themselves, along with a few other add-ins. This speeds up the process considerably, while still resulting in a tasty, crunchy, and very satisfying meal.

SERVES 4
PREP TIME: 10 minutes
COOK TIME: 20 minutes

3 tablespoons olive oil, plus more for the baking dish

6 large tomatoes

2 garlic cloves, minced

1 tablespoon chopped fresh parsley

½ cup pine nuts, finely ground

1 cup fine breadcrumbs (preferably from a bakery)

Sea salt

Freshly ground black pepper

1 Preheat the oven to 375°F. Lightly grease a 9-by-11-inch glass baking dish with olive oil.

2 Cut the stem ends off the tomatoes, use a teaspoon to remove the insides, and transfer to a cutting board. Take care not to break the walls of the tomatoes as you work. Set the tomatoes upside down to drain on some paper towels while you prepare the rest of the ingredients.

3 Mince the insides of the tomatoes and put them in a medium bowl. Add the 3 tablespoons of oil, the garlic, parsley, pine nuts, and breadcrumbs and mix well to combine. Season with salt and pepper.

4 Spoon the mixture into the hollow tomatoes. Carefully set them in the baking dish and bake for 15 to 16 minutes, until the topping is crunchy.

5 Turn the oven to broil for an additional 2 to 3 minutes to toast the tops. Serve hot or at room temperature.

VARIATION: To make this dish even more filling, reduce the breadcrumbs to only ½ cup, boil 1 cup instant rice for 5 minutes, and add it to the breadcrumb mixture. Stuff the tomatoes and bake as directed.

EGGPLANT PIZZAS

◇◇◇◇◇◇◇◇◇◇◇◇◇◇◇◇◇◇◇ PIZZETTE DI MELANZANE ◇◇◇◇◇◇◇◇◇◇◇◇◇◇◇◇◇◇◇

L ove the flavor of eggplant Parmesan but not the work involved? I don't blame you—neither do I! This dish takes all the flavors of the traditional Sicilian dish and reduces the work significantly. These lovely *pizzette* are perfect straight from the oven but also wonderful served at room temperature or even cold. This is a great way to get the kids to eat more vegetables; it's also a great family recipe.

SERVES 4
PREP TIME: 10 minutes
COOK TIME: 15 minutes

¾ cup fine breadcrumbs (preferably from a bakery)

2 tablespoons chopped fresh parsley

2 medium eggplants, cut crosswise into ¼-inch-thick rounds

Sea salt

Olive oil

1 cup canned crushed tomatoes

1 cup shredded mozzarella cheese

1 Preheat the oven to 400°F. Line a baking sheet with parchment paper.

2 In a shallow bowl, mix together the breadcrumbs and parsley.

3 Season the eggplant slices with salt and dip them into the breadcrumb mixture, patting the coating to stick to the eggplant. Place the slices on the prepared baking sheet.

4 Lightly drizzle some olive oil on the eggplant slices. Transfer to the oven and bake for 12 to 13 minutes, flipping them halfway through, until the coating is slightly browned on both sides.

5 Remove the pan from the oven. Top each slice with 1 to 2 teaspoons of the tomatoes and sprinkle on some mozzarella. Return to the oven for 2 to 3 minutes, until the cheese is bubbling and melted.

VEGETABLE KEBABS

◇◇◇◇◇◇◇◇◇◇◇◇◇◇◇◇◇◇◇◇◇◇ SPIEDINI DI VERDURE ◇◇◇◇◇◇◇◇◇◇◇◇◇◇◇◇◇◇◇◇◇◇◇

Growing up in Italy as the daughter of a greengrocer, I ate my share of vegetables. This particular combo is wonderful in the summer, when zucchini, eggplant, and tomatoes are at their peak. The vegetables cook quickly and are very colorful, making them the perfect choice when you're craving something healthy.

SERVES 4
PREP TIME: 15 minutes
COOK TIME: 15 minutes

2 medium zucchini, cut into ½-inch-thick rounds

1 pint cherry tomatoes

1 red bell pepper, cut into 1-inch squares

1 medium eggplant, cut into 1-inch cubes

8 ounces small white button mushrooms, stemmed

1 red onion, cut into thick slices

¼ cup olive oil

1 teaspoon Italian seasoning

Sea salt

Freshly ground black pepper

1 Preheat the oven to 400°F.

2 In a large bowl, combine the zucchini, tomatoes, bell pepper, eggplant, mushrooms, onion, oil, and Italian seasoning. Season with salt and black pepper. Use your hands or a wooden spoon to thoroughly mix everything so all the vegetables are well coated.

3 Thread the vegetables into wooden skewers and place them on a baking sheet. Continue until you have 6 to 8 kebabs.

4 Bake for 10 to 12 minutes, until the vegetables are softened. Serve hot or at room temperature.

INGREDIENT TIP: All the vegetables in this recipe have a high water content and will cook in about the same amount of time. Cutting the vegetables to about the same size will ensure they cook evenly.

EGGS IN PURGATORY

◇◇◇◇◇◇◇◇◇◇◇◇◇◇◇◇◇◇◇◇ UOVA IN PURGATORIO ◇◇◇◇◇◇◇◇◇◇◇◇◇◇◇◇◇◇◇◇

A specialty of southern Italy, *uova in purgatorio* is a go-to lunch or dinner when you want to keep cooking to an absolute minimum, but you still want something homemade, healthy, and delicious. Southerners add lots of red pepper flakes, but I must confess, I rarely do; I prefer a more subtle dish. It's uncertain where the name came from. Some claim that the egg white represents the purity of heaven, while the fiery red sauce represents the other side. Thus, the eggs are in between, in purgatory.

SERVES 4
PREP TIME: 5 minutes
COOK TIME: 15 minutes

2 tablespoons olive oil

¼ small yellow or white onion, finely diced

½ tablespoon chopped fresh basil

1 cup canned crushed tomatoes

Sea salt

Red pepper flakes (optional)

8 large eggs

1 In a medium skillet, combine the oil, onion, and basil and heat over medium heat for 1 minute, until the onion is slightly softened. Add the canned tomatoes, season with salt and pepper flakes (if using), reduce the heat to low, and cook the sauce for 7 to 8 minutes to thicken slightly.

2 Make 8 divots in the sauce using the back of a spoon and carefully crack one egg into each divot. Using a wooden spoon, gently swirl the whites and add a little bit of sauce on top of the yolk, taking care to not break the yolk. Cook the eggs for 3 to 5 minutes, until they are done the way you like.

3 Spoon the eggs into bowls or serving dishes and serve immediately.

PAIRING TIP: The tomato sauce in this dish is perfect for dunking ciabatta bread or even focaccia, so be sure to have some on hand for this quick dinner.

THREE-CHEESE FRITTATA

◇◇◇◇◇◇◇◇◇◇◇◇◇◇◇◇ FRITTATA TRE FORMAGGI ◇◇◇◇◇◇◇◇◇◇◇◇◇◇◇◇

Frittatas make the perfect weeknight dinner. They're quick and filling, and once you master the flipping process of stovetop frittatas, the flavor combinations are limited only by your imagination. Adding parsley to this frittata offers a hint of freshness and complements the ricotta very nicely.

SERVES 4
PREP TIME: 5 minutes
COOK TIME: 15 minutes

6 large eggs

¼ cup shredded low-moisture mozzarella cheese

2 ounces fresh mozzarella cheese, finely diced

½ cup whole-milk ricotta cheese

1 tablespoon finely chopped fresh parsley

Sea salt

Freshly ground black pepper

1 tablespoon olive oil

1 In a large bowl, vigorously whisk the eggs for 1 minute. Add the shredded mozzarella, diced fresh mozzarella, and ricotta and mix until all the ingredients are combined. Stir in the parsley and season with salt and pepper.

2 In a nonstick medium skillet, heat the oil over medium-low heat. Swirl the pan to coat with the oil. Add the egg mixture and cook for about 1 minute undisturbed, until the sides are slightly set.

3 Using a silicone spatula, swirl the eggs all around, and bring the edges of the eggs toward the center of the pan. This allows any liquid eggs in the center to flow toward the edges of the pan for even cooking. Continue this process of swirling the eggs and bringing any wet egg from the center to the edges for about 8 minutes. At this point, the frittata should be solidifying, while the center will still be slightly undercooked. Leave the frittata undisturbed for 2 or 3 minutes.

4 Find a plate with a larger diameter than the skillet. Place it over the pan and confidently invert the frittata onto the plate. Then slide the frittata back into the skillet, top-side down, and cook for 2 to 3 additional minutes, until it's firm. Invert again and serve.

INGREDIENT TIP: Whole-milk ricotta works best in this recipe. It provides the richness and creaminess that part-skim ricotta cannot offer.

SPINACH AND MOZZARELLA FRITTATA

◇◇◇◇◇◇◇◇◇◇◇◇ FRITTATA CON SPINACI E MOZZARELLA ◇◇◇◇◇◇◇◇◇◇◇◇

A frittata is a classic Italian egg dish served throughout the country. Unlike omelets, which are usually prepared in individual servings and served at breakfast, *frittate* are prepared in a large pan and usually serve 3 or 4 people. In Italy, they're mostly served at lunch and dinner, and not for breakfast. You can finish them in the oven, but that adds cooking time. Cooking from start to finish on the stovetop cuts the cooking time, and it's easier than you think.

SERVES 4 to 6
PREP TIME: 5 minutes
COOK TIME: 15 minutes

1 (12-ounce) bag baby spinach

8 large eggs

½ cup shredded mozzarella cheese

Sea salt

Freshly ground black pepper

1 tablespoon olive oil

1 Place the spinach in a medium skillet with no oil or water. Set the pan over medium heat and cook for 2 minutes, mixing with tongs as it cooks, until wilted. Drain any liquid from the pan and set the spinach aside.

2 In a large bowl, vigorously whisk the eggs for 1 minute. Add the mozzarella and season with salt and pepper. Give the cooked spinach a rough chop and add it to the egg mixture. Whisk to combine.

3 Using a paper towel, wipe down the skillet the spinach cooked in, add the oil, and heat over medium-low heat. Swirl the pan to coat it with the oil. Add the egg mixture and cook for about 1 minute undisturbed, until the sides are slightly set.

4 Using a silicone spatula, swirl the eggs all around and bring the edges of the eggs toward the center of the pan. This allows any liquid eggs in the center to flow toward the edges of the pan for even cooking. Continue this process of swirling the eggs and bringing any wet egg from the center to the edges for about 6 minutes. At this point, the frittata should be solidifying, while the center will still be slightly undercooked. Leave the frittata undisturbed for 2 minutes.

5 Find a plate with a larger diameter than the skillet. Place it over the pan and confidently invert the frittata onto the plate. Then slide the frittata back into the skillet, top-side down, and cook for 3 to 4 additional minutes, until it's firm. Invert again and serve.

INGREDIENT TIP: Stovetop frittatas can be intimidating, so if you're new to this process, start with this basic recipe with limited ingredients. The more you add, the heavier it will be, the more cooking time it will require, and the more difficult the inverting might be. This basic recipe, which is packed with flavor but minimal ingredients, is a great start.

PASTA ALLA NORMA

This is a typical Sicilian dish in that it's economical, hearty, and convenient and uses limited but high-quality ingredients. A specialty of the city of Catania, but enjoyed all over the island as well as on the mainland, this first course is often served with a bit of shaved ricotta salata cheese on top. Because that's not so readily available, I've substituted a tablespoon of fresh ricotta.

SERVES 4 to 6
PREP TIME: 10 minutes
COOK TIME: 20 minutes

¼ cup olive oil, plus
more as needed

2 medium eggplants,
cut into ½-inch cubes

Sea salt

Freshly ground black pepper

12 ounces penne, ziti, or
other tubular pasta

2 garlic cloves, minced

2 tablespoons chopped
fresh basil

1 (28-ounce) can
crushed tomatoes

4 to 6 tablespoons
whole-milk ricotta cheese

Grated Parmesan or Pecorino
Romano cheese (optional)

1 In a large sauté pan, heat the oil over medium heat. Add the eggplant. Season with salt and pepper. Cook for 5 to 7 minutes, until the eggplant is nicely browned all over, adding additional oil if needed. Transfer to a plate, leaving any leftover oil in the pan. If there is no leftover oil, add an additional tablespoon.

2 Meanwhile, in a 6-quart pot, bring 4 quarts of salted water to a boil over high heat. Add the pasta and cook according to the package directions.

3 Add the garlic and basil to the sauté pan that the eggplant was cooked in. Set over medium heat and cook for 1 minute, or until the garlic is golden but not burned. Add the tomatoes and season with salt and pepper. Cook the sauce for about 13 minutes, stirring occasionally, until it's slightly thickened.

4 Return the cooked eggplant to the sauce and mix. Drain the pasta and toss it with the tomato sauce in the pan.

5 Divide the pasta among bowls and serve with about 1 tablespoon of ricotta cheese on top. Top with grated cheese, if desired.

INGREDIENT TIP: Choose eggplants that have no blemishes and with a deep, dark skin. Keep in mind that eggplants soak up a lot of oil during cooking, so you'd prefer, you can also roast them for 10 minutes at 400°F instead of cooking them on the stovetop.

ORECCHIETTE WITH BROCCOLI RABE

⟡⟡⟡⟡⟡⟡⟡⟡ ORECCHIETTE CON LE CIME DI RAPA ⟡⟡⟡⟡⟡⟡⟡⟡

A specialty of the region of Puglia, especially the city of Bari, orecchiette are pasta shaped to resemble little earlobes. If you travel to Bari, you might find homemakers preparing these in front of their homes, all too willing to sell them to eager tourists to bring back home. In Puglia, they are most often served with broccoli rabe, red pepper flakes, garlic, and grated cheese, though other common combinations include chickpeas, green peas, and other similar vegetables. Homemade fresh orecchiette are often used in Bari, but store-bought dried are the perfect substitute.

SERVES 4
PREP TIME: 5 minutes
COOK TIME: 15 minutes

Sea salt

12 ounces orecchiette pasta

2 large bunches broccoli rabe, florets only

¼ cup olive oil, plus more for drizzling

2 garlic cloves, minced

Red pepper flakes

Grated Parmesan or pecorino cheese (optional)

1 In a 6-quart pot, bring 4 quarts of salted water to a boil over high heat. Add the orecchiette and cook according to the package directions (usually about 11 minutes). After the pasta has cooked for 3 to 4 minutes, add the broccoli rabe florets to the same pot and continue cooking together for an additional 7 to 8 minutes, taking care to not overcook the pasta.

2 Meanwhile, in a large sauté pan, heat the oil over medium heat. Add the garlic and pepper flakes and sauté for 2 to 3 minutes, until the garlic is golden but not burned.

3 Reserving about ¼ cup of the pasta water, drain the orecchiette and broccoli rabe and add them to the sauté pan. Add the pasta water and mix well to combine. Season with salt.

4 To serve, drizzle with some olive oil. If desired, top with grated cheese.

INGREDIENT TIP: Choose broccoli rabe that is a vibrant green and not at all wilted. If you see any yellowing of the florets, they are past their prime. Just the florets are used here, so reserve the stems and leaves for soups and stews.

ZITI WITH CREMINI MUSHROOMS

◇◇◇◇◇◇◇◇◇◇◇◇◇◇ ZITI CON FUNGHI CREMINI ◇◇◇◇◇◇◇◇◇◇◇◇◇◇

While mushrooms are enjoyed all over Italy, they are especially popular in the region of Piedmont and are used in many dishes. This pasta dish is perfect for fall, when the weather gets cooler and we all crave something warm and a bit heavier. And while southern Italians prefer to cook with olive oil, in the north they add a bit of butter to this and many other dishes.

SERVES 4 to 6
PREP TIME: 10 minutes
COOK TIME: 15 minutes

Sea salt

1 pound ziti or other tubular pasta

2 tablespoons olive oil

1 tablespoon unsalted butter

1 pound cremini mushrooms, sliced

1 garlic clove, minced

¼ cup dry white wine

Freshly ground black pepper

1 tablespoon chopped fresh basil

Grated Parmesan cheese (optional)

1 In a 6-quart pot, bring 4 quarts of salted water to a boil over high heat. Add the pasta, stir, and cook for 2 minutes less than the package directions.

2 Meanwhile, in a large sauté pan, heat the oil and butter over medium heat. Add the mushrooms, garlic, wine, and salt and pepper to taste. Cook for about 10 minutes, stirring occasionally, until the mushrooms have softened.

3 Reserving about ¼ cup of the pasta water, drain the pasta and add it to the sauté pan. Add the basil and continue cooking for several minutes, until the pasta is fully cooked. Add the reserved pasta water if you want a thicker sauce—the starch in the water will thicken it up.

4 Serve immediately. If desired, top with grated cheese.

SHORTCUT: For an even faster meal, purchase presliced mushrooms—they will save a bit of prep time.

ITALIAN SAUSAGES, PEPPERS, AND ONIONS, PAGE 85

CHAPTER 5

POULTRY AND MEAT MAINS

Classic Chicken Cutlets | *Cotolette di Pollo* 78

Chicken Florentine | *Pollo alla Fiorentina* 79

Chicken Piccata | *Piccata di Pollo* 80

Chicken Saltimbocca with Cherry Tomatoes |
Saltimbocca alla Romana con Pomodorini 81

Chicken Puttanesca | *Pollo Puttanesca* 82

Turkey Marsala | *Tacchino alla Marsala* 83

Calabrian-Style Turkey | *Tacchino alla Calabrese* 84

Italian Sausages, Peppers, and Onions |
Salcicce, Peperoni e Cipolle 85

Pork Chops in White Wine Sauce | *Fettine
di Maiale in Vino Bianco* 86

Pork Chops with Rosemary and Butter Sauce |
Fettine di Maiale al Rosmarino e Burro 87

Veal Milanese | *Cotolette alla Milanese* 88

Lamb Chops in Lemon and Caper Sauce |
Costolette con Salsa di Limone e Capperi 89

Steak Pizzaiola | *Bistecca alla Pizzaiola* 90

Beef Braciole | *Involtine di Carne in Bianco* 91

CLASSIC CHICKEN CUTLETS

◇◇◇◇◇◇◇◇◇◇◇◇◇◇◇◇◇◇◇ COTOLETTE DI POLLO ◇◇◇◇◇◇◇◇◇◇◇◇◇◇◇◇◇◇◇

I t doesn't get any more classic than chicken cutlets coated in egg wash and dipped in a mixture of breadcrumbs and lots of Parmesan. This dish is served all over Italy and is a favorite for families with young kids. While the classic is chicken, you can substitute veal cutlets, which cook in even less time, or turkey cutlets, which are usually a little bit thicker and require a few more minutes of cooking time. Panzanella (page 29) would make a nice *contorno* (side dish) for these fried cutlets.

SERVES 4
PREP TIME: 10 minutes
COOK TIME: 20 minutes

1 cup all-purpose flour

3 large eggs

2 cups fine breadcrumbs
(preferably from a bakery)

1 cup grated
Parmigiano-Reggiano cheese

8 thin-sliced chicken
breast cutlets

Sea salt

Freshly ground black pepper

Vegetable oil, for frying

1 Set up a dredging station with three medium bowls. Place the flour in one bowl. In the next bowl, lightly beat the eggs with a fork. In the third bowl, combine the breadcrumbs and Parmigiano and blend with a fork or your fingers.

2 Season the chicken with salt and pepper. Dredge each chicken cutlet in the flour, shaking off the excess. Next dip them in the eggs, holding them above the plate so the excess egg can drip off. Then add the chicken to the breadcrumb–cheese mixture and turn to coat evenly, patting the mixture with your hands to help it adhere to the chicken. Place the breaded cutlets on a plate.

3 Line a large plate with two layers of paper towels.

4 In a large sauté pan, add enough oil to fully submerge the cutlets (the exact amount depends on the size of your pan). Heat the oil over medium heat to 350°F. (If you don't have a thermometer, dip the end of a wooden spoon into the oil. If bubbles appear on the surface of the spoon, the oil is hot enough.)

5 Working in batches of 2 or 3, add the cutlets to the hot oil and cook for about 3 minutes per side, until the coating is golden brown all over. Transfer the cooked cutlets to the paper towels. Season with salt and serve hot.

CHICKEN FLORENTINE

Alla fiorentina ("in the Florentine style") often refers to recipes that contain spinach. This creamy dish is the perfect weeknight dinner. I add a bit of dry white wine, but if you don't have any on hand, add the same amount of stock instead. Add a cheese board with some ricotta, cubed Parmigiano-Reggiano, ciliegine (cherry-size) mozzarella balls, and focaccia as an antipasto for an even more satisfying meal.

SERVES 4
PREP TIME: 5 minutes
COOK TIME: 20 minutes

4 thin-sliced chicken breast cutlets

Sea salt

Freshly ground black pepper

½ cup all-purpose flour

3 tablespoons olive oil, divided

1 tablespoon unsalted butter

¼ small yellow or white onion, finely chopped

2 garlic cloves, finely minced

½ cup dry white wine

½ cup chicken or vegetable stock

1 (12-ounce) bag baby spinach

¾ cup heavy cream

1 Season the chicken with salt and pepper. Place the flour on a plate and dredge the cutlets in the flour on both sides, shaking off the excess. Discard any leftover flour.

2 In a large sauté pan, heat 2 tablespoons of oil over medium-low heat. Add the chicken and cook for about 4 minutes on each side, until the cutlets are lightly browned on both sides. Remove from the pan and set aside.

3 To the same pan, add the remaining 1 tablespoon of oil, the butter, onion, and garlic and cook for 1 minute, or until the garlic is slightly golden but not burned, scraping up any bits from the bottom of the pan.

4 Increase the heat to medium and add the wine and stock. Stir for 30 or so seconds. Add the spinach and cook down for about 2 minutes, or until it's wilted. Add the cream, mix well, and bring the cream to a boil, stirring constantly, 1 to 2 minutes.

5 Return the chicken to the pan and cook for 2 minutes to reheat it in the sauce. Remove from the heat and serve hot, spooning the sauce on top.

VARIATION: Turn this into a gluten-free dinner by skipping the flour. The final result will be a thinner sauce, but no less delicious.

CHICKEN PICCATA

PICCATA DI POLLO

Piccata refers to a dish in which meat is pounded flat (for easier and faster cooking) and served with a lemon and caper sauce, often made creamy by the addition of butter. Chicken is one of the most common meats used in a piccata, but you can substitute veal or turkey cutlets. And to save time, this starts with store-bought thin-sliced chicken cutlets so you don't have to pound them. This dish doesn't have any added veggies, but Leccese-Style Sweet Peppers (page 61) would pair nicely.

SERVES 4
PREP TIME: 5 minutes
COOK TIME: 20 minutes

4 thin-sliced chicken breast cutlets

Sea salt

Freshly ground black pepper

½ cup all-purpose flour

2 tablespoons unsalted butter, divided

2 tablespoons olive oil, divided

2 garlic cloves, finely minced

¾ cup chicken stock

Grated zest and juice of 1 lemon

2 tablespoons capers, rinsed

1 Season the chicken with salt and pepper. Place the flour on a plate and dredge the cutlets in the flour on both sides, shaking off the excess. Discard any leftover flour.

2 In a large sauté pan, heat 1 tablespoon of butter and 1 tablespoon of oil over medium-low heat. Add the chicken and cook for 4 minutes on each side, or until the chicken is lightly browned on both sides. Remove from the pan and set aside.

3 Increase the heat to medium and add the remaining 1 tablespoon each of butter and oil. Add the garlic, cook for 1 minute, and scrape up any bits that have stuck to the bottom of the pan. Add the stock, lemon zest, and lemon juice and cook the sauce for 5 minutes to slightly reduce and thicken. Stir in the capers.

4 Return the chicken to the pan and cook for 2 minutes to reheat in the sauce. Remove from the heat and serve hot, spooning the sauce on top.

VARIATION: This sauce works wonderfully with seafood, too. Swap the chicken for tilapia, use vegetable stock instead of chicken, and follow the recipe as written. Use a gentle hand when cooking tilapia, as it's delicate and tends to break down easily.

CHICKEN SALTIMBOCCA WITH CHERRY TOMATOES

◇◇◇◇◇◇◇◇ SALTIMBOCCA ALLA ROMANA CON POMODORINI ◇◇◇◇◇◇◇◇

*S*altimbocca alla romana is a classic dish from Rome now enjoyed all over the country. *Saltimbocca* translates to "jump in your mouth"—because this dish is so delicious it is said to jump in your mouth! This meal is quick, tasty, and impressive.

SERVES 4
PREP TIME: 5 minutes
COOK TIME: 20 minutes

4 thin-sliced chicken breast cutlets

Sea salt

Freshly ground black pepper

8 large fresh sage leaves

4 thin slices prosciutto

½ cup all-purpose flour

3 tablespoons olive oil, divided

4 tablespoons (½ stick) unsalted butter, divided

1 pint cherry tomatoes, halved

¾ cup chicken stock

1 Season the chicken with salt and pepper. Place 2 sage leaves on each of the chicken cutlets. Lay a slice of prosciutto over the sage.

2 Place the flour on a plate. Holding on to the prosciutto and chicken at the edge, dredge the cutlets in the flour on both sides, shaking off the excess. Discard any leftover flour.

3 In a large skillet, heat 2 tablespoons of oil and 2 tablespoons of butter over medium heat. Add the chicken cutlets, prosciutto-side down, and cook for about 5 minutes. Flip the chicken and cook for an additional 4 to 5 minutes, until the chicken is browned and cooked through. Remove from the pan and set aside.

4 Add the remaining 1 tablespoon of oil and 2 tablespoons of butter to the skillet. Add the cherry tomatoes and cook for 3 to 4 minutes, stirring occasionally, until they are softened and the skins begin to peel away from the flesh. Increase the heat to high, add the chicken stock, and bring to a boil. Cook for about 3 minutes, or until the sauce is reduced by half.

5 Return the chicken to the skillet prosciutto-side up. Reduce the heat to medium and simmer the chicken in the sauce for an additional 1 minute. Transfer the chicken to serving plates, pour the sauce over the top, and serve hot.

CHICKEN PUTTANESCA

POLLO PUTTANESCA

Puttanesca is a specialty of the city of Naples. The sauce is spicy, tangy, and carries a kick. Often served with pasta (see Spaghetti Puttanesca, page 49), it can also be delicious with other ingredients. Using boneless and skinless chicken thighs means everything cooks quickly and efficiently. And this one-pan dish makes cleanup a snap!

SERVES 4 to 6
PREP TIME: 5 minutes
COOK TIME: 25 minutes

8 boneless, skinless
chicken thighs

Sea salt

Freshly ground black pepper

3 tablespoons olive
oil, divided

2 garlic cloves, minced

3 anchovy fillets packed in oil

Red pepper flakes

1 (28-ounce) can
crushed tomatoes

¾ cup pitted black or
green olives, halved

1 Season the chicken with salt and pepper. In a large sauté pan, heat 2 tablespoons of oil over medium heat. Add the chicken thighs and cook for 3 minutes on each side, until they are lightly browned. Remove from the pan and set aside.

2 Add the remaining 1 tablespoon of oil to the pan and add the garlic, anchovies, and pepper flakes to taste. Cook for about 1 minute, using a wooden spoon to break down the anchovies until they're almost dissolved.

3 Add the tomatoes and olives to the pan and stir for 1 minute. Return the chicken to the pan and cook until the sauce is slightly thickened and the chicken is fully cooked through, about 15 minutes.

4 Serve the chicken hot with sauce spooned over the top.

PAIRING TIP: Round out this meal by using the sauce to also top some pasta!

TURKEY MARSALA

<><><><><><><><><><><><> TACCHINO ALLA MARSALA <><><><><><><><><><><><>

Marsala is a fortified Italian wine often used in poultry and veal dishes—and, because of its sweetness, in desserts. Chicken or turkey Marsala is a popular restaurant dish that sounds far more complicated to prepare than it actually is. It's impressive enough for company but easy enough for any weeknight.

SERVES 4
PREP TIME: 5 minutes
COOK TIME: 20 minutes

4 thinly sliced turkey breast cutlets

Sea salt

Freshly ground black pepper

½ cup all-purpose flour

3 tablespoons olive oil, plus more if needed

8 ounces white or cremini mushrooms, thinly sliced

¼ small yellow or white onion, finely diced

2 garlic cloves, minced

½ cup Marsala wine

½ cup chicken stock

1 If the turkey cutlets are thicker than ⅛ inch, pound them thinner. Season the turkey with salt and pepper. Place the flour on a plate and dredge the cutlets in it, shaking off the excess. Discard any leftover flour.

2 In a large skillet, heat the oil over medium heat. Add the turkey and cook for about 5 minutes per side, or until the cutlets are lightly golden all over. Remove them from the pan and set aside.

3 Reduce the heat to low and add the mushrooms, onion, and garlic and sauté for 5 minutes. Add an additional tablespoon of oil, if needed. Scrape up any bits that are stuck to the bottom of the pan. Add the Marsala and cook for about 1 minute, until it evaporates slightly. Add the stock, increase the heat to medium, and bring the sauce to a light boil, reducing the liquid slightly.

4 Return the turkey to the pan and simmer for an additional 1 minute to reheat. Serve the turkey hot with the sauce spooned over the top.

PAIRING TIP: A Pinot Noir will complement this dish perfectly. It's just right with the turkey and mushrooms, but not so overwhelming that it will overpower the sweetness of the Marsala.

CALABRIAN-STYLE TURKEY
TACCHINO ALLA CALABRESE

I must confess, growing up in Italy, I ate a lot of rabbit served in this style. Once we moved to the United States, we cooked chicken and turkey this way instead because good-quality rabbit was (and still is) hard to find. Using turkey cutlets in this recipe really cuts down on the cooking time. Unlike many recipes where the wine evaporates quickly at a high heat, in this dish the turkey and wine cook together for a good amount of time, ensuring that the turkey is really flavored with the wine. Round this dish out with some Vegetable Kebabs (page 67) for a very satisfying dinner.

SERVES 4
PREP TIME: 5 minutes
COOK TIME: 25 minutes

4 turkey breast cutlets

Sea salt

Freshly ground black pepper

3 tablespoons olive oil

½ medium yellow or white onion, diced

1 cup dry white wine

2 garlic cloves, finely minced

2 tablespoons chopped fresh basil

1 sprig fresh rosemary

1 teaspoon dried oregano

1 (14.5-ounce) can diced tomatoes

1 cup water

1 Season the turkey with salt and pepper. In a large sauté pan, heat the oil over medium heat. Add the turkey and onion to the pan and cook about 4 minutes, turning the turkey once, until it is lightly browned on both sides.

2 Add the wine and simmer for 8 to 10 minutes, reducing the heat if the wine is evaporating too quickly.

3 Add the garlic, basil, rosemary, and oregano and stir to combine. Add the tomatoes and water. Bring to a simmer and cook for about 10 minutes to thicken the sauce.

4 Discard the rosemary stem. Serve the turkey hot with the sauce spooned over the top.

VARIATION: This recipe is very versatile, so feel free to use any kind of meat. Boneless or bone-in chicken thighs and pork chops work very well cooked in this matter. The key is to make sure the meat cooks in the wine for a substantial period to really flavor it. Adding the onion is also key because it will release lots of water.

ITALIAN SAUSAGES, PEPPERS, AND ONIONS

SALCICCE, PEPERONI E CIPOLLE

An Italian staple served regionally, this dish is as classic Italian as they come. Although you can use all colors of bell peppers, I find red ones are sweeter and cook faster than the others. This is a wonderful family dish, adored by children and adults alike. You will often find it served by street food vendors during summer festivals.

SERVES 4
PREP TIME: 10 minutes
COOK TIME: 20 minutes

¼ cup olive oil, plus more if needed

3 red bell peppers, thinly sliced

2 small yellow or white onions, diced

1 tomato, chopped

2 tablespoons chopped fresh parsley

Sea salt

Freshly ground black pepper

2 teaspoons Italian seasoning

6 Italian sausages (sweet or hot), each cut into 5 or 6 pieces

1 In a large sauté pan or skillet, heat the oil over medium heat for 1 minute. Add the bell peppers, onions, tomato, and parsley. Season with salt and black pepper, add the Italian seasoning, and cook for 5 minutes, or until the peppers are slightly softened and the onion is a bit translucent. If the oil is absorbing too quickly, reduce the heat.

2 Add the sausages and cook, stirring, for 15 minutes. If the mixture looks dry, check the heat and adjust accordingly. Add a few additional tablespoons of olive oil if needed, or a few tablespoons of water.

3 Serve hot or at room temperature.

INGREDIENT TIP: Freezing the sausages for 1 hour before prepping will make dicing them easier.

VARIATION: Although cooking this on the stovetop is faster, you can also add all the ingredients to a baking dish and bake at 375°F for about 40 minutes. It's a wonderful alternative when you have a bit more time and don't want to stand at the stove.

PORK CHOPS IN WHITE WINE SAUCE
◇◇◇◇◇◇◇◇◇◇ FETTINE DI MAIALE IN VINO BIANCO ◇◇◇◇◇◇◇◇◇◇

While the northerners focus more on beef, pork is the meat of choice of many living in southern Italy, especially Calabria. I love making this because it's flavorful and versatile. What follows is a very basic version of the dish, but you could add some lemon juice, capers, olives, and other herbs. You could also cook lamb chops in the same method, and they would be equally delicious. Some light and simple Genovese-Style Spinach (page 60) would go very well next to these wonderful chops.

SERVES 4
PREP TIME: 5 minutes
COOK TIME: 20 minutes

4 bone-in pork chops

Sea salt

Freshly ground black pepper

2 tablespoons olive oil, divided

3 garlic cloves, minced

½ small yellow or white onion, diced

1 cup dry white wine

¾ cup chicken or vegetable stock

1 teaspoon all-purpose flour

1 tablespoon chopped fresh parsley

1 Season the pork chops with salt and pepper. In a large skillet, heat 1 tablespoon of the oil over medium heat. Add the pork chops and cook for 3 to 4 minutes per side, until they're lightly browned on both sides. Remove from the pan and set aside.

2 Add the remaining 1 tablespoon of oil to the pan. Add the garlic and onion and cook for about 2 minutes, or until they are slightly browned but not burned.

3 Increase the heat to high and add the wine and stock, stirring to scrape up any of the bits that are stuck to the pan. Sift the flour on top and stir to cook and dissolve the flour. Cook for 3 to 4 minutes, until the sauce is thickened and reduced by half.

4 Return the pork chops to the pan to reheat for 2 minutes. Serve hot with the parsley and sauce spooned on top.

PORK CHOPS WITH ROSEMARY AND BUTTER SAUCE

◇◇◇◇◇◇◇◇◇ FETTINE DI MAIALE AL ROSMARINO E BURRO ◇◇◇◇◇◇◇◇◇

I t's very common in northern Italy to add cream and butter to many dishes. Unlike in the south, where cooks thrive on putting extra-virgin olive oil on just about anything, northern Italians enjoy heavier cream and butter sauces. Each region makes use of what they most have available, which is the beauty of Italian cuisine. Northerners have more cattle, while southerners have more olive trees, so it's not a mystery why each region cooks the way it does.

SERVES 4
PREP TIME: 10 minutes
COOK TIME: 20 minutes

4 bone-in pork chops

Sea salt

Freshly ground black pepper

2 tablespoons olive oil

1 small yellow or white onion, chopped

12 ounces cremini mushrooms, thinly sliced

1 sprig fresh rosemary

½ cup heavy cream

2 tablespoons unsalted butter

1 Season the pork chops with salt and pepper. In a large sauté pan or skillet, heat the oil over medium heat. Add the pork chops and cook for 3 to 4 minutes per side, until they're browned on both sides. Remove from the pan and set aside.

2 Reduce the heat to medium-low, add the onion, mushrooms, and rosemary, and cook for about 3 minutes, or until the onion is translucent and softened.

3 Add the cream and butter and season with salt and pepper. Return the pork chops to the pan and cook for an additional 4 to 5 minutes, until the sauce is thickened. Serve hot with the sauce spooned on top.

VEAL MILANESE

◇◇◇◇◇◇◇◇◇◇◇◇◇ COTOLETTE ALLA MILANESE ◇◇◇◇◇◇◇◇◇◇◇◇◇

A classic recipe from the city of Milan, this dish is utterly decadent, as it's cooked only in butter. The dish calls for just a few ingredients, but all play a very important role in creating a rich, buttery cutlet. The veal chop is pounded to a ½-inch thickness so it cooks quickly. Reduce the cooking time if you'd prefer a medium-rare chop. Serve this on its own or with Oven-Roasted Stuffed Tomatoes (page 65).

SERVES 4
PREP TIME: 5 minutes
COOK TIME: 15 minutes

2 large eggs

Sea salt

Freshly ground black pepper

4 bone-in veal chops

1½ cups fine breadcrumbs (preferably from a bakery)

7 tablespoons unsalted butter

Lemon wedges (optional)

1 In a medium bowl, lightly beat the eggs with a fork. Season with salt and pepper. Line a large plate with paper towels.

2 Avoiding the bone, pound the meat of the veal chops until it is about ½ inch thick. Dip the chops in the beaten eggs, then dip them into the breadcrumbs, avoiding the bone. Press the breadcrumbs to better adhere to the meat.

3 In a large sauté pan or skillet, heat the butter for 3 to 4 minutes, until the butter is golden but not burned. Working in batches if necessary, cook the veal chops for 4 to 5 minutes per side. If the chops are browning too quickly, reduce the heat to medium.

4 Transfer the chops to the paper towels to drain for 1 minute before serving. If desired, serve with lemon wedges for squeezing.

PAIRING TIP: Veal is delicate, so even though this dish is cooked in butter, you want to select a wine that isn't too overwhelming. A light red, such as a Pinot Noir, will work wonderfully because it's not too bold.

LAMB CHOPS IN LEMON AND CAPER SAUCE

⬦⬦⬦⬦⬦⬦⬦⬦ COSTOLETTE CON SALSA DI LIMONE E CAPPERI ⬦⬦⬦⬦⬦⬦⬦⬦

L emons and capers seem to go hand in hand and are often paired to create lemony sauces. Lamb chops also go very well with anything lemon. Lamb can taste gamey, but the addition of ingredients with bold flavors, such as wine, stock, and lemons, balances that unique taste.

SERVES 4
PREP TIME: 10 minutes
COOK TIME: 20 minutes

4 bone-in lamb chops

Sea salt

Freshly ground black pepper

2 tablespoons olive oil

2 tablespoons unsalted butter

½ small yellow or white onion, chopped

2 garlic cloves, minced

1 cup dry white wine

1 cup vegetable stock

Juice of 1 lemon

2 tablespoons capers, drained

1 Season the lamb chops with salt and pepper. In a large sauté pan or skillet, heat the oil over medium heat. Add the chops and cook 3 to 4 minutes per side, until they're browned on both sides. Work in batches if the pan is not big enough to accommodate the four chops. Remove from the pan and set aside.

2 Drain any fat left in the pan and add the butter. Add the onion and garlic and cook for 1 minute. Increase the heat to medium-high, add the wine, stock, and lemon juice, and bring to a slight boil. Cook for about 5 minutes, or until thickened and reduced by about half.

3 Add the capers to the pan, then return the chops and cook for an additional 2 to 3 minutes to reheat and fully cook them through. Serve hot with the sauce on top.

PAIRING TIP: The rich and strong flavor of lamb is best paired with an equally rich and strong red wine, such as a bold Chianti.

STEAK PIZZAIOLA

BISTECCA ALLA PIZZAIOLA

Alla pizzaiola typically refers to dishes that use tomatoes and oregano—ingredients often found on pizza. It's a method of cooking that Neapolitans are known for, and they cook many dishes in this style. Rib-eye steaks are ideal for cooking *alla pizzaiola* because they are tender and absorb the flavors of tomatoes and oregano perfectly.

SERVES 4
PREP TIME: 5 minutes
COOK TIME: 15 minutes

2 tablespoons olive
oil, divided

4 rib-eye steaks (4 to
6 ounces each)

Sea salt

Freshly ground black pepper

2 garlic cloves, minced

1 teaspoon dried oregano

1 cup canned crushed
tomatoes

1 In a large sauté pan or skillet, heat a light drizzle of oil over medium heat. Season the steaks with salt and pepper and cook for about 3 minutes per side, or until browned on both sides. Transfer the steaks to a plate.

2 Wipe out the pan with paper towels and set over low heat. Add the remaining olive oil, the garlic, and oregano and cook for 1 minute. Add the tomatoes, season with salt, and cook for about 7 minutes to slightly thicken the sauce.

3 Return the steaks to the pan and nestle them in the sauce to reheat for 1 minute. Serve hot, with the sauce spooned on top.

BEEF BRACIOLE

◇◇◇◇◇◇◇◇◇◇◇◇◇◇ INVOLTINE DI CARNE IN BIANCO ◇◇◇◇◇◇◇◇◇◇◇◇◇◇

Braciole refers to thin slices of meat (usually beef), or even vegetables, that are rolled around a stuffing of some type; the roll-ups are also referred to as *involtine*. These tender bites of deliciousness are the perfect weeknight dinner. Requiring just a few ingredients, they cook fast, are tender, and please all the picky eaters in the household.

SERVES 4 to 6
PREP TIME: 5 minutes
COOK TIME: 15 minutes

8 thinly sliced beef sirloin steaks (sometimes sold as braciola)

Sea salt

Freshly ground black pepper

8 thin slices deli-style provolone

8 thin slices pancetta

¼ cup grated Parmigiano-Reggiano cheese

3 tablespoons olive oil

1 cup dry white wine

1   Season the meat with salt and pepper. On each slice of meat, add 1 slice of provolone and 1 slice of pancetta. Sprinkle a pinch of Parmigiano on top and roll up the meat slices tightly, paying close attention to the sides to ensure they're closed. Stick a wooden toothpick in the seams of each roll-up to keep them closed, or use some kitchen twine to tie them closed.

2   In a large sauté pan or skillet, heat the oil over medium heat. Add the beef roll-ups and brown for 5 minutes, turning to evenly brown them on all sides.

3   Reduce the heat to low, add the wine, season with additional salt and pepper, and stir. Cover the pan and cook the braciole for about 10 minutes, or until fully cooked. Serve hot.

VARIATION: Serving any dish *in bianco* means without adding tomatoes, but this dish is also wonderful *rosso*, meaning with tomatoes. Add 1 cup of canned crushed tomatoes after adding the wine; the end result will be a lovely tomato sauce, which is great for mopping up with some crusty bread.

SAUTÉED MUSSELS AND CLAMS, PAGE 96

CHAPTER 6

SEAFOOD MAINS

Pasta with Tuna, Tomatoes, and Olives |
Pasta con Tonno, Pomodorini e Ulive **94**

Mixed Fish Fry | *Fritto Misto di Mare* **95**

Sautéed Mussels and Clams | *Sauté di Cozze e Vongole* **96**

Mussels au Gratin | *Cozze Gratinate* **97**

Shrimp fra Diavolo | *Scampi fra Diavolo* **98**

Shrimp in White Wine and Lemon Sauce |
Scampi in Vino Bianco e Succo di Limone **99**

Pizzaiola-Style Scallops | *Capesante alla Pizzaiola* **100**

Neapolitan-Style Cod | *Baccalà alla Napolitana* **101**

Swordfish Kebabs | *Spiedini di Pesce Spada* **102**

PASTA WITH TUNA, TOMATOES, AND OLIVES

◇◇◇◇◇◇◇◇◇◇ PASTA CON TONNO, POMODORI E ULIVE ◇◇◇◇◇◇◇◇◇◇

Italian tuna packed in olive oil is a staple ingredient in my pantry that I use in countless ways. This dish is similar to a pasta salad, and it's wonderful served hot or at room temperature. Feel free to add some capers in step 3; they lend saltiness and a bit of tang.

SERVES 4
PREP TIME: 10 minutes
COOK TIME: 15 minutes

Sea salt

12 ounces penne, ziti, or other tubular pasta

2 (5.5-ounce) cans tuna packed in olive oil, drained, oil reserved

2 tablespoons olive oil, plus more if needed

½ small yellow or white onion, chopped

5 anchovy fillets packed in oil, roughly chopped

1 pint cherry tomatoes, halved

¼ cup chopped pitted black olives

2 tablespoons chopped fresh parsley

½ cup dry white wine

1 In a 6-quart pot, bring 4 quarts of salted water to a boil over high heat. Add the pasta and cook to 2 minutes less than the package directions.

2 Meanwhile, in a large sauté pan, combine the drained oil from the tuna, the olive oil, and onion. Set over medium heat and cook for 2 minutes, or until the onion is softened and slightly translucent. Add the anchovies and cook for 1 to 2 minutes, until they almost melt into the oil.

3 Add the tuna, tomatoes, olives, and parsley. Increase the heat to high and sauté for 3 minutes. Add the wine and let it evaporate for 2 minutes.

4 Reserving about ½ cup of the pasta water, drain the pasta and add it to the sauce. Mix well to combine, adding a little more olive oil if needed. Add some pasta water if it seems too dry.

5 Cook the pasta with the sauce for 2 minutes to fully incorporate the flavors of the sauce. Taste and season with salt. Serve hot or at room temperature.

INGREDIENT TIP: The anchovies and olives both pack some salt, as does the pasta cooked in salted water. That's why I recommend waiting to season with added salt until the end. Taste the final dish and adjust as needed.

MIXED FISH FRY

<><><><><><><><><><><><><><> FRITTO MISTO DI MARE <><><><><><><><><><><><><><>

Fritto misto di mare is a beloved southern Italian dish that uses a bounty of seafood. Surrounded by the ocean, regions such as Calabria, Sicily, and Puglia make use of what is most readily available. This dish is best enjoyed hot, right out of the oil, so prepare it just before serving. Coat the fish in the flour immediately before frying so the flour will not have time to moisten and get soggy; you'll end up with a crunchier coating.

SERVES 4 to 6
PREP TIME: 15 minutes
COOK TIME: 10 minutes

Sunflower oil or vegetable oil, for deep-frying

½ pound small sea scallops

16 large peeled and deveined shrimp

1 pound cleaned squid, bodies sliced into rings (see Tip)

½ pound cod, cut into 2- to 3-inch cubes

Sea salt

Freshly ground black pepper

2 cups all-purpose flour

Lemon wedges, for serving

INGREDIENT TIP: If you're a fan of squid tentacles (some people aren't), include them here. Fry then after you're done frying the rings.

1 Fill a large sauté pan or deep-fryer three-quarters full with oil and heat the oil to 350°F. (If you don't have a thermometer, dip the end of a wooden spoon into the oil. If bubbles appear on the surface of the wood, the oil is hot enough.) Line a large dish with paper towels.

2 While the oil is heating, season the scallops, shrimp, squid, and cod with salt and pepper. Add the flour to a large bowl and dredge the seafood in the flour, shaking off the excess. Discard any leftover flour.

3 Add the seafood to the hot oil (take care not to splatter) in separate batches in this order: First, scallops and shrimp, which will cook in less than 1 minute. Then the squid, which will fry in just about 1½ minutes. End with the cod, which will cook in 2 to 3 minutes, depending on the thickness; the outside will be golden. When the seafood is cooked, remove from the hot oil with a slotted spoon and drain on the paper towels.

4 Transfer everything to a clean plate, season with salt, and serve with lemon wedges.

PAIRING TIP: A Sauvignon Blanc is the perfect wine to pair with fried seafood. It's crisp, light, and fruity and complements seafood wonderfully.

SAUTÉED MUSSELS AND CLAMS

◇◇◇◇◇◇◇◇◇◇◇◇◇ SAUTÉ DI COZZE E VONGOLE ◇◇◇◇◇◇◇◇◇◇◇◇◇

This is a staple dish in southern Italy, where seafood is plentiful and eaten year round. This dish cooks extremely quickly—scrubbing and cleaning the shells is more time-consuming than the actual cooking. It's great served as a main dish or a starter. If you want to add some pasta, the broth left in the pan should be enough to cook about half a pound. Thin, long pasta such as spaghetti or angel hair go particularly well with this recipe.

SERVES 4 to 6
PREP TIME: 15 minutes
COOK TIME: 10 minutes

½ cup olive oil

4 garlic cloves, minced

2 tablespoons chopped fresh parsley

1 pint cherry tomatoes, halved

1½ pounds mussels, rinsed and debearded

1½ pounds clams, rinsed and scrubbed clean

Sea salt

Freshly ground black pepper

1 cup dry white wine

Crusty bread (optional)

1 In a large sauté pan, heat the oil over medium heat. Add the garlic and cook for 1 minute, or until it's slightly golden but not burned. Add the parsley and tomatoes and stir.

2 Add the mussels and clams and stir to combine. Season with salt and pepper. Cover with a lid and cook undisturbed for 2 minutes. Add the white wine, stir, and cover again. Cook for 3 to 4 minutes, stirring occasionally. Remove the lid and check to see if the mussels and clams have opened up (as soon as they open up, you can assume they are cooked). Continue cooking for an additional minute if any remain unopened. Discard any mussels and clams that remain closed after 7 minutes of cooking.

3 Serve hot in bowls. If desired, accompany with crusty bread to dunk in the sauce.

VARIATION: This is a wonderful base recipe for mussels and clams. Additions may include olives, capers, lemon juice, fresh herbs, and red pepper flakes. Mix things up according to your preference.

MUSSELS AU GRATIN

◇◇◇◇◇◇◇◇◇◇◇◇◇◇◇◇◇◇◇◇◇ COZZE GRATINATE ◇◇◇◇◇◇◇◇◇◇◇◇◇◇◇◇◇◇◇◇◇

Quick, delicious, and with a hint of crunch, mussels au gratin are a wonderful option for a weeknight dinner when you want something delicious and healthy but time is of the essence. This is another staple served in Calabria, Sicily, and Puglia, where the surrounding oceans offer a bounty of fresh seafood. Be sure to spend a few minutes scrubbing the mussels clean and pulling out any noticeable beard.

SERVES 4 to 6
PREP TIME: 10 minutes
COOK TIME: 10 minutes

2 tablespoons olive
oil, divided

2 pounds mussels,
cleaned and debearded

½ cup dry white wine

1 cup fine breadcrumbs
(preferably from a bakery)

2 garlic cloves, minced

Juice of ½ lemon

1 tablespoon white
wine vinegar

2 tablespoons chopped
fresh parsley

Sea salt

PAIRING TIP: The perfect accompaniment would be a green salad made with endive, fennel, and scallions, topped with olives, capers, and anchovies, and dressed with extra-virgin olive oil and lemon juice.

1 Preheat the broiler or preheat the oven to 450°F.

2 In a large sauté pan, heat 1 tablespoon of olive oil over medium heat for 30 seconds, until it's just slightly warmed. Add the mussels and white wine, cover with a lid, and cook for 5 to 7 minutes, until the mussels open up. Discard any that remain closed after 7 minutes of cooking.

3 Meanwhile, in a small bowl, combine the breadcrumbs, garlic, lemon juice, vinegar, parsley, and the remaining 1 tablespoon of olive oil. Season with salt and mix with a fork until the breadcrumbs are moistened and well mixed.

4 Remove the mussels from the heat and remove and discard the top halves of the shells (leaving the mussel meat in the other half).

5 Arrange the mussels on the half shell on a large baking sheet and spoon 1 to 2 teaspoons of the breadcrumb mixture on top of each mussel. Broil or bake for 2 minutes, or until the breadcrumbs are browned and crunchy. Serve immediately.

VARIATION: To mix things up, you can follow the same recipe using clams instead of mussels.

SHRIMP FRA DIAVOLO

<><><><><><><><><><><> SCAMPI FRA DIAVOLO <><><><><><><><><><><><><><><>

F*ra diavolo* means "deviled" in Italian, so you can bet that any recipe with this name is going to be spicy! But feel free to modify this southern Italian recipe according to your taste buds. You can easily control the heat by adding or subtracting red pepper flakes. The typical amount in this dish is about 1 teaspoon, but I have left out a specific measurement so you can season it to your liking.

SERVES 4
PREP TIME: 5 minutes
COOK TIME: 15 minutes

Sea salt

12 ounces spaghetti, linguini, angel hair, or other long, thin pasta

2 tablespoons olive oil, divided

1 pound peeled and deveined large shrimp

2 garlic cloves, minced

Red pepper flakes

2 tablespoons chopped fresh parsley

2 cups canned crushed tomatoes

1 In a 6-quart pot, bring 4 quarts of salted water to a boil over high heat. Add the pasta and cook according to the package directions.

2 Meanwhile, in a large sauté pan, heat 1 tablespoon of oil over medium heat until it's just slightly warmed. Add the shrimp and sauté for 3 minutes, or until they turn pink and are cooked through. Remove from the heat and set aside.

3 Add the remaining 1 tablespoon of oil to the pan and add the garlic, pepper flakes to taste, and the parsley. Sauté for 1 minute, or until the garlic is golden but not burned. Add the tomatoes, season with salt, and cook for 7 minutes to slightly thicken the sauce.

4 Return the shrimp to the pan to reheat for 1 minute. Drain the pasta and add to the sauté pan. Stir until everything is combined. Serve hot.

PAIRING TIP: Because this dish carries such a punch, a wine that is not too overpowering will be ideal, such as a Pinot Grigio or Sauvignon Blanc.

SHRIMP IN WHITE WINE AND LEMON SAUCE

×◇×◇×◇×◇×◇× SCAMPI IN VINO BIANCO E SUCCO DI LIMONE ×◇×◇×◇×◇×◇×

This quick, simple, light meal is the perfect option for those nights when you have only a few minutes to spare in the kitchen. The shrimp are cooked when they change color to light pink or light orange, which usually happens after they have been on the heat for just a few minutes. Lemon complements seafood dishes really well on its own, but when paired with wine the resulting sauce is even more tempting. Cook some angel hair pasta for a more substantial meal.

SERVES 4
PREP TIME: 5 minutes
COOK TIME: 10 minutes

3 tablespoons olive oil

2 garlic cloves, minced

Grated zest and juice of 1 lemon

1 pound peeled and deveined large shrimp

Sea salt

Freshly ground black pepper

2 tablespoons chopped fresh parsley

1 cup dry white wine

1 In a large sauté pan, heat the oil over medium heat. Add the garlic and lemon zest and cook for 1 minute, or until the garlic is golden but not burned.

2 Season the shrimp with salt and pepper and add to the pan, along with the parsley. Cook for about 3 minutes, stirring occasionally, until the shrimp turn pink and are fully cooked through.

3 Add the wine and lemon juice and heat for 2 minutes, or until the wine evaporates and the liquid is slightly reduced. Serve immediately.

SHORTCUT: Buying shrimp that is already peeled and deveined eliminates substantial preparation time for shrimp dishes. Most major grocery stores sell shrimp that has already been cleaned.

PIZZAIOLA-STYLE SCALLOPS

CAPESANTE ALLA PIZZAIOLA

Scallops, and many other types of seafood, are the perfect weeknight option because of their quick cooking time. Here, they are prepared alla pizzaiola, meaning the dish is going to have a good amount of oregano, tomatoes, and basil—all ingredients typically found on pizza. A favorite from the city of Naples, the key in this dish is to leave the scallops undisturbed as they sear on the hot oil. This will result in a golden outer crust.

SERVES 4
PREP TIME: 5 minutes
COOK TIME: 15 minutes

Sea salt

12 ounces angel hair pasta

4 tablespoons olive oil, divided

1 pound medium scallops

Freshly ground black pepper

2 garlic cloves, minced

3 tablespoons chopped fresh basil

1 teaspoon dried oregano

¼ cup dry white wine

2 cups canned crushed tomatoes

1 In a 6-quart pot, bring 4 quarts of salted water to a boil over high heat. Add the pasta and cook for 1 minute less than the package directions.

2 Meanwhile, in a large sauté pan, heat 2 tablespoons of olive oil over medium-high heat for 2 minutes. Season the scallops with salt and pepper and add to the hot pan. Do not disturb the scallops for 2 minutes, then flip them and sear on the other side undisturbed for an additional 2 minutes. Remove them from the pan and set aside.

3 Reduce the heat to medium and add the remaining 2 tablespoons of oil, the garlic, basil, oregano, and wine. Deglaze the pan by scraping up any bits that have stuck from the scallops and allow the wine to evaporate for 1 minute. Add the tomatoes, stir, and cook for 5 to 6 minutes to slightly thicken the sauce.

4 Return the scallops to the sauce to reheat for 1 minute. Drain the pasta and add it to the sauté pan. Toss to combine. Serve hot.

NEAPOLITAN-STYLE COD

⬦⬦⬦⬦⬦⬦⬦⬦⬦⬦⬦⬦⬦⬦ BACCALÀ ALLA NAPOLITANA ⬦⬦⬦⬦⬦⬦⬦⬦⬦⬦⬦⬦⬦⬦

Baccalà alla napolitana is a spicy seafood dish from the city of Naples. Traditionally served on Christmas Eve, when many Italians abstain from eating meat, this dish certainly packs a punch from the red pepper flakes, capers, and olives. The amount of red pepper flakes is completely up to you, and you could omit them altogether for a milder taste. In Italy, this dish is made with both fresh cod and salt cod, which has to be soaked in water for several days before you can cook with it. Obviously several days of soaking doesn't work for a quick recipe, so this is the fresh cod version of the dish.

SERVES 4 to 6
PREP TIME: 5 minutes
COOK TIME: 20 minutes

2 tablespoons olive oil

2 garlic cloves, minced

2 tablespoons chopped fresh parsley

1 (28-ounce) can crushed tomatoes

Red pepper flakes

1 teaspoon dried oregano

1 cup water

2 tablespoons capers, rinsed

½ cup pitted and halved black olives

1½ pounds cod loin fillet, cut into 4- to 5-inch portions

Sea salt

1 In a large sauté pan (large enough to hold the fish without crowding), heat the oil over medium-low heat for 30 seconds. Add the garlic and parsley and cook for 1 minute, or until the garlic is slightly golden but not burned. Add the crushed tomatoes, pepper flakes to taste, the oregano, and water. Cook the sauce for 10 minutes to slightly thicken. Add the capers and olives and mix well.

2 Gently add the fish to the sauce. With a wooden spoon, cover the fish with some of the sauce. Simmer the fish in the sauce for 12 to 15 minutes, until the cod is tender and begins to flake. Check on the fish a few times while cooking to make sure it's not drying out too quickly. If it is, reduce the heat to low and add several tablespoons of water.

3 Taste the sauce and season with salt as needed. The capers and olives will provide some saltiness. Serve hot.

PAIRING TIP: Pair this dish with some cooked pasta. Cook and drain the pasta and toss with some of the sauce. Serve the fish on top or in a separate dish.

SWORDFISH KEBABS

SPIEDINI DI PESCE SPADA

Swordfish is thick, fleshy, and meaty, making it the ideal seafood to roast, bake, or grill. Swordfish is widely served in Calabria, where it's freshly caught and prepared immediately upon catching. Serve this alongside a simple green salad and you have the perfect dinner.

SERVES 4
PREP TIME: 5 minutes
COOK TIME: 15 minutes

1 pound swordfish, cut into 1½-inch cubes

Sea salt

Freshly ground black pepper

¼ cup olive oil

Grated zest and juice of 1 lemon

2 garlic cloves, minced

2 tablespoons finely chopped fresh parsley

2 tablespoons finely chopped fresh basil

1 teaspoon dried oregano

1 Preheat the oven to 400°F.

2 Season the swordfish with salt and pepper. Place in a medium bowl.

3 In a small bowl, combine the oil, lemon zest, lemon juice, garlic, parsley, basil, and oregano. Mix with a fork to combine. Pour the marinade over the swordfish and mix to fully coat and season the fish.

4 Thread the swordfish cubes onto 4 to 6 skewers and set them in a baking dish. Pour any remaining marinade over the fish. Bake for 14 to 15 minutes, until the fish is opaque. Serve hot.

SHORTCUT: Don't have skewers on hand, or want to save a few extra minutes of preparation? Skip making the kebabs and simply transfer the fish chunks to a baking dish.

LIMONCELLO TIRAMISU, PAGE 112

CHAPTER 7

SWEET DRINKS AND DESSERTS

Dark Chocolate Affogato | *Affogato al Caffè con Cioccolato* 106

White Peach and Raspberry Bellini |
Bellini di Pesca Bianca con Lamponi 107

Lemon and Mint Sgroppino | *Sgroppino al Limone con Mente* 108

Mixed Fresh Fruit Salad | *Macedonia di Frutta* 109

Warm Peaches with Chocolate and Crushed Amaretti |
Pesche con Cioccolato e Amaretti 110

Classic Ricotta Cannoli | *Cannoli alla Ricotta* 111

Limoncello Tiramisu | *Tiramisù al Limoncello* 112

Easy Espresso Tiramisu Dip | *Crema a Gusto di Tiramisù* 114

DARK CHOCOLATE AFFOGATO

◇◇◇◇◇◇◇◇◇◇◇ AFFOGATO AL CAFFÈ CON CIOCCOLATO ◇◇◇◇◇◇◇◇◇◇◇

The word *affogato* means "drowned" in Italian, and in this sweet afterdinner drink it refers to vanilla gelato being drowned in a bit of freshly brewed espresso. The ingredients are few, but the end result is pure heaven. Although it's served all over Italy, southern Italians seem to have a particular love for this dessert. It's the perfect combination of hot and cold, all in one.

SERVES 4
PREP TIME: 5 minutes
COOK TIME: 5 minutes

1 cup freshly brewed
hot espresso

1 tablespoon sugar

2 pints vanilla gelato

1 ounce dark chocolate,
finely minced

1 Brew the espresso on the stovetop or in a French press coffee maker. Add the sugar and mix until it's dissolved.

2 Place 2 scoops of gelato in each of four serving bowls or glasses. Divide the hot espresso among the serving bowls, top with minced chocolate, and serve immediately.

PAIRING TIP: A few dry almond biscotti will be the perfect accompaniment to this dessert. Serve on the side or dipped in the serving glass.

WHITE PEACH AND RASPBERRY BELLINI

<><><><><><><><> BELLINI DI PESCA BIANCA CON LAMPONI <><><><><><><><>

Born in Venice, Italy, in 1948 at the world-famous Harry's Bar, the Bellini is arguably one of the most famous cocktails in Italy. It's sweet, fruity, and enjoyed by everyone who has ever had the pleasure of sipping one. Usually served in a tall champagne flute, it can be a cocktail before dinner but is sweet enough to be served for dessert. It's also perfect with brunch. This simple drink is sure to become your next favorite.

SERVES 2
PREP TIME: 5 minutes

2 white peaches,
peeled and pitted

1½ cups chilled Prosecco

Fresh raspberries

Fresh mint leaves

1 In a blender, purée the peaches for 30 to 45 seconds. Divide the purée between two champagne flutes or serving glasses.

2 Top up the champagne flutes with the Prosecco. Garnish with a few raspberries and a mint leaf and serve immediately.

VARIATION: Replace the peach purée with mandarin juice to make a Puccini, or make a Rossini by replacing the peach purée with strawberry purée. And if you use pomegranate juice instead of the peach purée, you have a Tintoretto!

LEMON AND MINT SGROPPINO

 SGROPPINO AL LIMONE CON MENTE

Another specialty from the Veneto region, this lemony drink is the perfect cocktail to start a meal, to end it, or even to serve between courses to cleanse the palate. It also makes a great dessert drink—almost like an adult shake.

SERVES 2
PREP TIME: 5 minutes

1 cup chilled Prosecco

2 tablespoons chilled vodka

½ cup lemon sorbet

2 teaspoons sugar (optional)

Fresh mint leaves

1 In a small bowl, combine the Prosecco, vodka, sorbet, and sugar (if using) and gently whisk with a fork to combine.

2 Divide between two champagne flutes. Garnish with mint leaves and serve.

PAIRING TIP: Pair this drink with some crunchy biscotti or amaretti cookies.

MIXED FRESH FRUIT SALAD

◇◇◇◇◇◇◇◇◇◇◇◇◇◇◇◇◇◇ MACEDONIA DI FRUTTA ◇◇◇◇◇◇◇◇◇◇◇◇◇◇◇◇◇◇

I talians love fruit for dessert, and summertime is the peak season for a wonderful fruit *macedonia*. There is no cooking involved, so the bulk of your time will be spent cutting up the mixed fruits. Although there is no exact recipe for this, I think the proposed combination that follows works perfectly. This is best served the same day it is prepared; by the next day, the fruits will have released some of their juices, making the dish a bit soggy and discolored.

SERVES 4 to 6
PREP TIME: 20 minutes

2 peaches, peeled and cubed

2 nectarines, peeled and cubed

1 pint strawberries, halved

2 cups cubed cantaloupe

2 cups cubed honeydew melon

Juice of ½ lemon

Juice of 1 orange

2 to 3 tablespoons honey

2 cups frozen whipped topping (see Tip, page 114), thawed

1 In a large serving bowl, combine the peaches, nectarines, strawberries, cantaloupe, honeydew, and lemon juice and mix well. Add the orange juice and honey and mix well. Taste for sweetness and adjust as needed by adding more honey if necessary.

2 Serve immediately, topped with a generous tablespoon of whipped topping.

INGREDIENT TIP: While almost all fruits work well in a fruit *macedonia*, there are two I would avoid: bananas and watermelon. Bananas turn dark and unsightly soon after peeling, and they become very soft and soggy when mixed with other fruits. And watermelon is just too watery: Its juices pool at the bottom of the bowl, causing the other fruits to become dark and soggy.

WARM PEACHES WITH CHOCOLATE AND CRUSHED AMARETTI

◇◇◇◇◇◇◇◇◇◇◇◇◇ PESCHE CON CIOCCOLATO E AMARETTI ◇◇◇◇◇◇◇◇◇◇◇◇◇

This is the perfect dessert for when you need something sweet, seasonal, and relatively healthy—for a dessert, anyway. This southern Italian staple is often served in the summer, when peaches are plentiful. A scoop of vanilla gelato is sure to perfectly complement the warmth of the peaches.

SERVES 4
PREP TIME: 5 minutes
COOK TIME: 20 minutes

¼ cup packed light or dark brown sugar

1 cup crushed amaretti cookies (8 to 10 cookies)

1 teaspoon vanilla extract

4 large peaches, halved and pitted

2 tablespoons unsalted butter

2 ounces dark chocolate

1 pint vanilla gelato

1 Position an oven rack in the center and preheat the oven to 400°F.

2 In a medium bowl, combine the brown sugar, amaretti crumbs, and vanilla and use a fork to mix thoroughly. Set the crumble aside.

3 Set the peach halves cut-side up in a baking dish or sheet pan. Spoon about 1 tablespoon of the amaretti crumble in the hollow left by the peach pit and use your fingers to pack it in. Add a small dab of butter on each peach half.

4 Transfer to the oven and bake for about 15 minutes, or until the peach flesh is softened. Turn the oven to broil and broil the peaches for 1 to 2 minutes, until the crumble is toasted.

5 As the peaches bake, add the chocolate to a small microwave-safe bowl and microwave in 30-second increments, stirring after each, until it's melted.

6 Remove the peaches from the oven, place on a serving dish, and drizzle on the chocolate. Serve with scoops of vanilla gelato.

SHORTCUT: You can prepare the crumble up to a few hours in advance, so when you're ready to bake, simply pit the peaches, add the crumble to each half, and bake.

CLASSIC RICOTTA CANNOLI
CANNOLI ALLA RICOTTA

A classic Sicilian dessert, cannoli are tubes of fried dough filled with a smooth and creamy mixture of ricotta cheese. Purchasing premade shells saves hours of time in the kitchen, and when you don't have to fry the shells, cleanup is a snap. There are several options online for different size shells; you can also check your local grocery store's bakery department. Because the filling is made from only a few ingredients, purchase the best ricotta you can find, made from whole milk.

SERVES 8
PREP TIME: 15 minutes

½ cup heavy whipping cream

½ cup powdered sugar, plus more for dusting

4 cups whole-milk ricotta cheese

8 large cannoli shells

8 maraschino cherries, halved (optional)

½ cup mini chocolate chips (optional)

1 In a medium bowl, with an electric mixer with the whisk attachment, whip the cream and powdered sugar until stiff peaks form, 3 to 4 minutes.

2 Use a rubber spatula to gently fold the ricotta into the whipped cream. Mix just until combined; do not overmix.

3 Using a pastry bag or a plastic freezer bag with the bottom corner cut off, pipe the cream into the shells. If desired, you can decorate the cannoli with a half maraschino cherry at one or both ends, or dip one or both ends into the chocolate chips, or mix and match the cherries and chocolate. Set on a serving platter and dust with powdered sugar. Serve immediately.

INGREDIENT TIP: Cannoli shells are best filled immediately before serving, so prepare the cream when you're done with dinner and ready to serve dessert. You can refrigerate the filled cannoli for up to 1 day, but expect the shells to get a bit soggy. Maraschino cherries and mini chocolate chips make excellent additions to this dessert, but chopped pistachios would also work wonderfully.

LIMONCELLO TIRAMISU
TIRAMISÙ AL LIMONCELLO

The traditional espresso tiramisu is a classic dessert from the Veneto region, although it's served and enjoyed all over Italy. The limoncello version is a newer take from the Amalfi Coast, an area that's bountiful in lemons and Italy's largest limoncello producer. This dish is refreshing, light, and the perfect ending to any summer meal.

SERVES 6 to 8
PREP TIME: 20 minutes
COOK TIME: 5 minutes

FOR THE FILLING

1 pound mascarpone cheese

⅓ cup store-bought lemon curd

¼ cup limoncello

Grated zest and juice of 1 lemon

1 cup heavy cream

⅓ cup powdered sugar

FOR THE SOAK

¾ cup granulated sugar

Grated zest and juice of 2 lemons

½ cup water

1 cup limoncello

1 **TO MAKE THE FILLING:** In a stand mixer with the whisk (or in a bowl with a handheld mixer), cream together the mascarpone, lemon curd, limoncello, lemon zest, and lemon juice. Beat for 1 minute until well blended. Set the mascarpone mixture aside.

2 In another bowl, with the electric mixer and whisk attachment, beat together the heavy cream and powdered sugar on high speed until stiff peaks form, 2 to 3 minutes.

3 Using a rubber spatula, fold the whipped cream into the mascarpone mixture, doing so gently so as not to deflate the whipped cream. Set aside.

4 **TO MAKE THE SOAK:** In a small saucepan, combine the granulated sugar, lemon zest, lemon juice, and water and bring to a boil. Mix gently with a fork or whisk and cook for about 2 minutes, or until the sugar is fully dissolved. Remove from the heat and stir in the limoncello.

FOR ASSEMBLY

30 to 35 ladyfingers

5 **TO ASSEMBLE THE TIRAMISU:** Taking one ladyfinger at a time, gently dip the cookie in the limoncello soak for 5 to 10 seconds per side. Arrange the ladyfingers in a 9-by-11-inch serving dish. Continue until you have a full layer of soaked ladyfingers. You can break them in half to fit the corners.

6 Spoon half the cream filling over the moistened ladyfingers and spread evenly all across the layer.

7 Dip the remaining ladyfingers and arrange them over the cream layer. Add the remaining cream and again, spread it evenly over the top.

8 Enjoy immediately, or refrigerate for 1 to 2 hours to enhance the flavor.

> **SHORTCUT:** To save a little time in this recipe, you can use an 8-ounce container of thawed frozen whipped topping instead of making whipped cream.

EASY ESPRESSO TIRAMISU DIP

◇◇◇◇◇◇◇◇◇◇◇◇◇◇◇◇◇ CREMA A GUSTO DI TIRAMISÙ ◇◇◇◇◇◇◇◇◇◇◇◇◇◇◇◇◇

Ideal for social gatherings or for a super-easy weeknight dessert, this dip is perfect to end any meal or simply for a sweet afternoon snack. The unmistakable flavor of mascarpone and espresso go together beautifully with the ladyfingers, which are the cookies traditionally used in tiramisu.

SERVES 4 to 6
PREP TIME: 10 minutes

1 pound mascarpone cheese

¼ cup freshly brewed espresso, cooled

½ cup powdered sugar

1 (8-ounce) container frozen whipped topping, thawed (see Tip)

Shaved chocolate (optional)

24 ladyfingers

1 In a stand mixer with the whisk (or in a bowl with a handheld mixer), whisk the mascarpone, espresso, and powdered sugar on low speed for 1 to 2 minutes.

2 Using a rubber spatula, gently fold in the whipped topping and mix until combined. Transfer to a serving bowl. If desired, top with some shaved chocolate.

3 Serve the cream with ladyfingers for dipping.

VARIATION: While this cream makes the perfect dip for ladyfingers, it's also wonderful as a filling or frosting alternative on homemade chocolate cupcakes. Use a piping bag to fill them, or simply smear some cream on top in place of frosting.

INGREDIENT TIP: If you'd prefer, make homemade whipped cream with 1 cup heavy whipping cream and ⅓ cup powdered sugar.

MEASUREMENT CONVERSIONS

VOLUME EQUIVALENTS (LIQUID)

US STANDARD	US STANDARD (OUNCES)	METRIC (APPROX.)
2 tablespoons	1 fl. oz.	30 mL
¼ cup	2 fl. oz.	60 mL
½ cup	4 fl. oz.	120 mL
1 cup	8 fl. oz.	240 mL
1½ cups	12 fl. oz.	355 mL
2 cups or 1 pint	16 fl. oz.	475 mL
4 cups or 1 quart	32 fl. oz.	1 L
1 gallon	128 fl. oz.	4 L

OVEN TEMPERATURES

FAHRENHEIT (F)	CELSIUS (C) (APPROX.)
250°	120°
300°	150°
325°	165°
350°	180°
375°	190°
400°	200°
425°	220°
450°	230°

VOLUME EQUIVALENTS (DRY)

US STANDARD	METRIC (APPROX.)
⅛ teaspoon	0.5 mL
¼ teaspoon	1 mL
½ teaspoon	2 mL
¾ teaspoon	4 mL
1 teaspoon	5 mL
1 tablespoon	15 mL
¼ cup	59 mL
⅓ cup	79 mL
½ cup	118 mL
⅔ cup	156 mL
¾ cup	177 mL
1 cup	235 mL
2 cups or 1 pint	475 mL
3 cups	700 mL
4 cups or 1 quart	1 L

WEIGHT EQUIVALENTS

US STANDARD	METRIC (APPROX.)
½ ounce	15 g
1 ounce	30 g
2 ounces	60 g
4 ounces	115 g
8 ounces	225 g
12 ounces	340 g
16 ounces or 1 pound	455 g

RESOURCES

BOOKS

Ball, Serena, RD, and Deranna Segrave-Daly, RD. *The 30-Minute Mediterranean Diet Cookbook: 101 Easy, Flavorful Recipes for Lifelong Health.* Rockridge Press, 2018.

Bastianich, Lidia Matticchio. *Lidia's Favorite Recipes: 100 Foolproof Italian Dishes, from Basic Sauces to Irresistible Entrees.* Knopf, 2012.

De Laurentiis, Giada. *Everyday Italian: 125 Simple and Delicious Recipes.* Clarkson Potter, 2005.

Montillo, Francesca. *Pasta in a Pinch: Classic and Creative Recipes Made with Everyday Pantry Ingredients.* Rockridge Press, 2020.

Montillo, Francesca. *The 5-Ingredient Italian Cookbook: 101 Regional Classics Made Simple.* Rockridge Press, 2018.

Viviani, Fabio. *Fabio's 30-Minute Italian: Over 100 Fabulous, Quick and Easy Recipes.* St. Martin's Press, 2017.

BLOGS

THE ITALIAN DISH

theitaliandishblog.com

With wonderful photography, creative recipes, and some videos, this website is great for visual folks who love seeing beautiful images of what a final dish should look like. From appetizers to soups to pasta and desserts, this is a great resource for everyone from novice cooks to experienced chefs.

LAZY ITALIAN CULINARY ADVENTURES

thelazyitalian.com/blog

This is a great resource for additional recipes requiring 30 to 45 minutes of prepping and cooking. The recipes are a mix of authentic and inventive, providing lots of options for dinnertime. A wonderful variety of dessert recipes can also be found here. For those interested in learning more about Italy itself, you will also find blog articles on distinctive locations and their history.

OUR ITALIAN TABLE

ouritaliantable.com

Managed by a brother-and-sister team, this beautifully written blog is full of festive recipes arranged by Italian regions. Informative, with gorgeous images and even the option to buy a number of authentic items from Italy, this is a site not to be missed.

INDEX

A

Acquacotta Toscana, 26
Affogato al Caffè con Cioccolato, 106
Amaretti, Crushed, and Chocolate,
 Warm Peaches with, 110
Anchovies, 10
 Calabrian-Style Penne, 45
 Chicken Puttanesca, 82
 Pasta with Tuna, Tomatoes,
  and Olives, 94
 Spaghetti Puttanesca, 49
Antipasti, guide to, 4–5
Antipasto Salad, 32–33
Artichoke hearts, 10

B

Baccalà alla Napolitana, 101
Balsamic vinegar, 13
Basil, 6
 Caprese-Style Tortellini Salad, 31
 Cavatelli with Broccoli Pesto, 47
 Pesto Pasta Salad, 30
 Ravioli with Tomato-
  Basil Sauce, 40
Beans, 10
 frozen Italian green beans, 11
 Green Beans and Potato Mash, 63
 Pasta and Bean Soup, 25
 Vegetable Minestrone, 24
Beef
 Beef Braciole, 91
 Quick Meat Sauce with
  Fettuccine, 51
 Steak Pizzaiola, 90
*Bellini di Pesca Bianca con
 Lamponi*, 107
Bistecca alla Pizzaiola, 90

Black pepper, 12
Bouillon cubes, 12
Bread
 Panzanella, 29
 Tuscan Bread and
  Tomato Soup, 23
 Tuscan Soup, 26
Breadcrumbs, 9
Broccoli Pesto, Cavatelli with, 47
Broccoli Rabe, Orecchiette with, 73

C

Calabrian-Style Penne, 45
Calabrian-Style Turkey, 84
Cannoli alla Ricotta, 111
Capers
 Chicken Piccata, 80
 Lamb Chops in Lemon
  and Caper Sauce, 89
 Leccese-Style Sweet Peppers, 61
 Neapolitan-Style Cod, 101
Capesante alla Pizzaiola, 100
Caprese-Style Tortellini Salad, 31
Cavatelli con Pesto di Broccoli, 47
Cheese
 for antipasto platter, 4
 Antipasto Salad, 32–33
 Beef Braciole, 91
 Caprese-Style Tortellini Salad, 31
 Cheesy Polenta with
  Sautéed Greens, 57
 Classic Chicken Cutlets, 78
 Classic Ricotta Cannoli, 111
 Creamy Gnocchi with
  Gorgonzola and
  Walnuts, 42–43
 Easy Espresso Tiramisu Dip, 114

Eggplant Pizzas, 66
Imperial Soup, 28
Italian Rice Salad, 34
Limoncello Tiramisu, 112–113
mozzarella, about, 9
Parmigiano-Reggiano,
 about, 8
Pecorino Romano, about, 8
Penne with Ham and Peas
 in Cream Sauce, 44
ricotta, about, 8
Roman Egg Drop Soup, 22
Spinach and Mozzarella
 Frittata, 70–71
Three-Cheese Frittata, 69
Chicken
 Chicken Florentine, 79
 Chicken Piccata, 80
 Chicken Puttanesca, 82
 Chicken Saltimbocca with
  Cherry Tomatoes, 81
 Classic Chicken Cutlets, 78
 Mamma's Classic Pastina, 27
Chickpeas, 10
Chocolate
 Dark Chocolate Affogato, 106
 Warm Peaches with Chocolate
  and Crushed Amaretti, 110
Clams
 Sautéed Mussels and Clams, 96
 Spaghetti in Clam Sauce, 50
Classic Chicken Cutlets, 78
Classic Ricotta Cannoli, 111
Cod
 Mixed Fish Fry, 95
 Neapolitan-Style Cod, 101
Colander, 15

Costolette con Salsa di Limone e Capperi, 89
Cotolette alla Milanese, 88
Cotolette di Pollo, 78
Cozze Gratinate, 97
Crackers, for antipasto platter, 4
Creamy Gnocchi with Gorgonzola and Walnuts, 42–43
Crema a Gusto di Tiramisù, 114
Crostini, for antipasto platter, 4
Cutting board, 15

D

Dark Chocolate Affogato, 106
Deli meats
  buying and storing, 7
  for antipasto platter, 4
  Italian Rice Salad, 34
Desserts
  Classic Ricotta Cannoli, 111
  Easy Espresso Tiramisu Dip, 114
  Limoncello Tiramisu, 112–113
  Mixed Fresh Fruit Salad, 109
  Warm Peaches with Chocolate and Crushed Amaretti, 110
Dip, Easy Espresso Tiramisu, 114
Drinks
  Dark Chocolate Affogato, 106
  Lemon and Mint Sgroppino, 108
  White Peach and Raspberry Bellini, 107
Dutch oven, 16

E

Easy Espresso Tiramisu Dip, 114
Eggplant
  Eggplant Pizzas, 66
  Pasta alla Norma, 72
  Rigatoni with Vegetarian Ragù, 48
  Vegetable Kebabs, 67
Eggs, 8
  Eggs in Purgatory, 68
  Imperial Soup, 28
  Italian Rice Salad, 34
  Roman Egg Drop Soup, 22
  Spinach and Mozzarella Frittata, 70–71

Three-Cheese Frittata, 69
Tuscan Soup, 26
Equipment, 15–17
Espresso
  Dark Chocolate Affogato, 106
  Easy Espresso Tiramisu Dip, 114

F

Fagioli Verdi con Patate, 63
Fettine de Maiale al Rosmarino e Burro, 87
Fettine de Maiale in Vino Bianco, 86
Fettuccine con Ragù Veloce di Carne, 51
Fish. *See* Seafood
Food processor, 17
Frittata con Spinaci e Mozzarella, 70–71
Frittata Tre Formaggi, 69
Fritto Misto di Mare, 95
Fruit. *See also* specific fruits
  dried, for antipasto platter, 5
  Mixed Fresh Fruit Salad, 109
Funghi Ripieni, 64

G

Garlic, 7
  Chicken Puttanesca, 82
  Leccese-Style Sweet Peppers, 61
  Scapece-Style Zucchini, 62
  Stuffed Mushroom Caps, 64
Garlic press, 17
Gelato
  Dark Chocolate Affogato, 106
  Warm Peaches with Chocolate and Crushed Amaretti, 110
Genovese-Style Spinach, 60
Gnocchi Cremosi con Gorgonzola e Noci, 42–43
Green beans
  Green Beans and Potato Mash, 63
  Italian, frozen, 11
Greens. *See also* Spinach
  Cheesy Polenta with Sautéed Greens, 57

H

Ham. *See also* Prosciutto
  Italian Rice Salad, 34
  Penne with Ham and Peas in Cream Sauce, 44
Herbs. *See also* specific herbs
  dried, 12
  fresh, freezing, 9
  Italian dried herb blend, 12

I

Imperial Soup, 28
Insalata Antipasto, 32–33
Insalata di Riso, 34
Insalata di Pasta con Pesto, 30
Insalata di Tortellini in Stile Caprese, 31
Insalata Panzanella, 29
Involtine di Carne in Bianco, 91
Italian cooking
  eating culture, 2
  equipment for, 15–17
  ingredients for, 6–13
  regional cuisines, 2–3
Italian Rice Salad, 34
Italian Sausages, Peppers, and Onions, 85

J

Jams, for antipasto platter, 5

K

Kebabs
  Swordfish Kebabs, 102
  Vegetable Kebabs, 67
Knives, 16

L

Ladyfingers
  Easy Espresso Tiramisu Dip, 114
  Limoncello Tiramisu, 112–113
Lamb Chops in Lemon and Caper Sauce, 89
Leccese-Style Sweet Peppers, 61

Lemons
  Chicken Piccata, 80
  Lamb Chops in Lemon
    and Caper Sauce, 89
  Lemon and Mint Sgroppino, 108
  Limoncello Tiramisu, 112–113
  Shrimp in White Wine and
    Lemon Sauce, 99
Limoncello Tiramisu, 112–113

M

Macedonia di Frutta, 109
Mamma's Classic Pastina, 27
Mandoline, 17
Meat. *See also* Beef; Lamb;
    Pork; Veal
  for antipasto platter, 4
  deli, buying and storing, 7
  deli, for antipasto platter, 4
  freezing, 9
  for recipes, 8
Minestra di Pasta e Fagioli, 25
Minestra di Verdure, 24
Mint
  Lemon and Mint
    Sgroppino, 108
  Scapece-Style Zucchini, 62
Mixed Fish Fry, 95
Mixed Fresh Fruit Salad, 109
Mixing bowls, 16
Mostaccioli in Salsa Rosa, 46
Mushrooms, 7
  Mushroom Risotto, 52
  Polenta with Sautéed
    Mushrooms, 56
  Pork Chops with Rosemary
    and Butter Sauce, 87
  Rigatoni with Vegetarian
    Ragù, 48
  Stuffed Mushroom Caps, 64
  Turkey Marsala, 83
  Vegetable Kebabs, 67
  Ziti with Cremini
    Mushrooms, 74
Mussels
  Mussels au Gratin, 97
  Sautéed Mussels and Clams, 96

N

Neapolitan-Style Cod, 101
Nuts. *See also* Pine nuts; Walnuts
  for antipasto platter, 5

O

Oils, 13
Olive oils, 13
Olives, 11
  Antipasto Salad, 32–33
  Calabrian-Style Penne, 45
  Chicken Puttanesca, 82
  Neapolitan-Style Cod, 101
  Panzanella, 29
  Pasta with Tuna, Tomatoes,
    and Olives, 94
  Spaghetti Puttanesca, 49
Onions
  Italian Sausages, Peppers,
    and Onions, 85
  storing, 7
Orecchiette con le Cime de Rapa, 73
Oregano, 12
Oven-Roasted Stuffed Tomatoes, 65

P

Pancetta
  Beef Braciole, 91
  Risotto with Peas and
    Pancetta, 54
Panzanella, 29
Pappa al Pomodoro, 23
Parsley, 7
Pasta, 10
  Calabrian-Style Penne, 45
  Caprese-Style Tortellini Salad, 31
  Cavatelli with Broccoli Pesto, 47
  Creamy Gnocchi with
    Gorgonzola and
    Walnuts, 42–43
  frozen stuffed, 12
  Mamma's Classic Pastina, 27
  Mostaccioli in Pink Sauce, 46
  Orecchiette with Broccoli
    Rabe, 73
  Pasta alla Norma, 72

Pasta and Bean Soup, 25
Pasta with Tuna, Tomatoes,
    and Olives, 94
Penne with Ham and Peas
    in Cream Sauce, 44
Pesto Pasta Salad, 30
Pizzaiola-Style Scallops, 100
Quick Meat Sauce with
    Fettuccine, 51
Ravioli in Butter and
    Sage Sauce, 39
Ravioli with Tomato-
    Basil Sauce, 40
Rigatoni with Vegetarian Ragù, 48
Shrimp fra Diavolo, 98
Spaghetti in Clam Sauce, 50
Spaghetti Puttanesca, 49
Tortellini in Broth, 41
Ziti with Cremini Mushrooms, 74
*Pasta con Tonno, Pomodori
    e Ulive*, 94
Pastina, 10
Pastina di Mamma, 27
Peaches
  Mixed Fresh Fruit Salad, 109
  Warm Peaches with Chocolate
    and Crushed Amaretti, 110
  White Peach and Raspberry
    Bellini, 107
Peas
  frozen, 12
  Penne with Ham and Peas
    in Cream Sauce, 44
  Risotto with Peas and
    Pancetta, 54
Peelers, 16
Penne, Panna e Prosciutto, 44
Penne alla Calabrese, 45
Peperoncini, 13
Peperoni Leccese, 61
Peppers, 7
  Antipasto Salad, 32–33
  Italian Sausages, Peppers,
    and Onions, 85
  Leccese-Style Sweet Peppers, 61
  Polenta with Sausage
    and Peppers, 55

Rigatoni with Vegetarian
　　Ragù, 48
roasted red, in jars, 11
Vegetable Kebabs, 67
Pesche con Cioccolato e
　　Amaretti, 110
Pesto
　　Cavatelli with Broccoli
　　　　Pesto, 47
　　Pesto Pasta Salad, 30
Piccata di Pollo, 80
Pickles, for antipasto platter, 5
Pine nuts
　　Genovese-Style Spinach, 60
　　Oven-Roasted Stuffed
　　　　Tomatoes, 65
Pizzaiola-Style Scallops, 100
Pizzette di Melanzane, 66
Polenta
　　Cheesy Polenta with
　　　　Sautéed Greens, 57
　　instant, 10
　　Polenta with Sausage
　　　　and Peppers, 55
　　Polenta with Sautéed
　　　　Mushrooms, 56
Polenta con Funghi Saltate, 56
Polenta con Salsicce e
　　Peperoni, 55
Polenta con Verdure Saltate, 57
Pollo alla Fiorentina, 79
Pollo Puttanesca, 82
Pomodori Ripieni al Forno, 65
Pork. *See also* Ham;
　　Pancetta; Sausages
　　Pork Chops in White
　　　　Wine Sauce, 86
　　Pork Chops with Rosemary
　　　　and Butter Sauce, 87
Potato and Green Beans
　　Mash, 63
Poultry. *See also* Chicken; Turkey
　　for recipes, 8
Prosciutto
　　Antipasto Salad, 32–33
　　Chicken Saltimbocca with
　　　　Cherry Tomatoes, 81

Q
Quick Meat Sauce with
　　Fettuccine, 51

R
Raisins
　　Genovese-Style Spinach, 60
Raspberry and White
　　Peach Bellini, 107
Ravioli con Salsa di Pomodori
　　e Basilico, 40
Ravioli in Burro e Salvia, 39
Recipes
　　labels, 18–19
　　notes, 18–19
　　tips, 19
Red pepper flakes, 13
Red wine vinegar, 13
Rice, 10
　　Italian Rice Salad, 34
　　Mushroom Risotto, 52
　　Risotto Milanese, 53
　　Risotto with Peas and
　　　　Pancetta, 54
Rigatoni con Ragù Vegetariano, 48
Risotto alla Milanese, 53
Risotto con Funghi, 52
Risotto con Piselli e Pancetta, 54
Roman Egg Drop Soup, 22
Rosemary and Butter Sauce,
　　Pork Chops with, 87

S
Saffron
　　Risotto Milanese, 53
Sage
　　Chicken Saltimbocca with
　　　　Cherry Tomatoes, 81
　　Ravioli in Butter and
　　　　Sage Sauce, 39
Salads
　　Antipasto Salad, 32–33
　　Caprese-Style Tortellini Salad, 31
　　Italian Rice Salad, 34
　　Mixed Fresh Fruit Salad, 109
　　Panzanella, 29

Pesto Pasta Salad, 30
Salami
　　Italian Rice Salad, 34
Salcicce, Peperoni e Cipolle, 85
Salt, 13
Saltimbocca alla Romana
　　con Pomodorini, 81
Sausages, 8–9
　　Italian Rice Salad, 34
　　Italian Sausages, Peppers,
　　　　and Onions, 85
　　Pesto Pasta Salad, 30
　　Polenta with Sausage
　　　　and Peppers, 55
Sauté di Cozze e Vongole, 96
Sautéed Mussels and Clams, 96
Sauté pans and skillets, 16
Scallops
　　Mixed Fish Fry, 95
　　Pizzaiola-Style Scallops, 100
Scampi fra Diavolo, 98
Scampi in Vino Bianco e
　　Succo di Limone, 99
Scapece-Style Zucchini, 62
Seafood, 9. *See also* Anchovies
　　Antipasto Salad, 32–33
　　frozen, 12
　　Italian Rice Salad, 34
　　Italian tuna packed in oil, 11
　　Mixed Fish Fry, 95
　　Mussels au Gratin, 97
　　Neapolitan-Style Cod, 101
　　Pasta with Tuna, Tomatoes,
　　　　and Olives, 94
　　Pizzaiola-Style Scallops, 100
　　Sautéed Mussels and Clams, 96
　　Shrimp fra Diavolo, 98
　　Shrimp in White Wine and
　　　　Lemon Sauce, 99
　　Spaghetti in Clam Sauce, 50
　　Swordfish Kebabs, 102
Sgroppino al Limone con
　　Mente, 108
Sheet pans, 16
Shrimp
　　Mixed Fish Fry, 95
　　Shrimp fra Diavolo, 98

Shrimp(*continued*)
  Shrimp in White Wine and
    Lemon Sauce, 99
Slotted and wooden spoons, 16
Sorbet
  Lemon and Mint Sgroppino, 108
Soup pot, 16
Soups
  Imperial Soup, 28
  Mamma's Classic Pastina, 27
  Pasta and Bean Soup, 25
  Roman Egg Drop Soup, 22
  Tuscan Bread and
    Tomato Soup, 23
  Tuscan Soup, 26
  Vegetable Minestrone, 24
Spaghetti alle Vongole, 50
Spaghetti in Clam Sauce, 50
Spaghetti Puttanesca, 49
Spiedini di Pesce Spada, 102
Spiedini di Verdure, 67
Spinach
  Antipasto Salad, 32–33
  Cheesy Polenta with
    Sautéed Greens, 57
  Chicken Florentine, 79
  Genovese-Style Spinach, 60
  Spinach and Mozzarella
    Frittata, 70–71
  Tortellini in Broth, 41
  Vegetable Minestrone, 24
Spinaci Genovese, 60
Squid
  Mixed Fish Fry, 95
Stracciatella alla Romana, 22
Stuffed Mushroom Caps, 64
Swordfish Kebabs, 102

T
Tacchino alla Calabrese, 84
Tacchino alla Marsala, 83
Three-Cheese Frittata, 69
Tiramisù al Limoncello, 112–113
Tiramisu Dip, Easy Espresso, 114
Tomatoes, 7
  Antipasto Salad, 32–33
  Calabrian-Style Penne, 45
  Calabrian-Style Turkey, 84

canned crushed, 11
canned diced, 11
canned whole peeled, 11
Caprese-Style Tortellini Salad, 31
Chicken Puttanesca, 82
Chicken Saltimbocca with
  Cherry Tomatoes, 81
Eggplant Pizzas, 66
Eggs in Purgatory, 68
Mostaccioli in Pink Sauce, 46
Neapolitan-Style Cod, 101
Oven-Roasted Stuffed
  Tomatoes, 65
Panzanella, 29
Pasta alla Norma, 72
Pasta and Bean Soup, 25
Pasta with Tuna, Tomatoes,
  and Olives, 94
Pesto Pasta Salad, 30
Pizzaiola-Style Scallops, 100
Polenta with Sausage
  and Peppers, 55
Quick Meat Sauce with
  Fettuccine, 51
Ravioli with Tomato-
  Basil Sauce, 40
Rigatoni with Vegetarian Ragù, 48
Sautéed Mussels and Clams, 96
Shrimp fra Diavolo, 98
Spaghetti Puttanesca, 49
Steak Pizzaiola, 90
Tuscan Bread and
  Tomato Soup, 23
Tuscan Soup, 26
Vegetable Kebabs, 67
Tortellini
  Caprese-Style Tortellini Salad, 31
  Tortellini in Broth, 41
Tortellini in Brodo, 41
Tuna
  Antipasto Salad, 32–33
  Italian, packed in oil, 11
  Italian Rice Salad, 34
  Pasta with Tuna, Tomatoes,
    and Olives, 94
Turkey
  Calabrian-Style Turkey, 84
  Turkey Marsala, 83

Tuscan Bread and Tomato Soup, 23
Tuscan Soup, 26

U
Uova in Purgatorio, 68

V
Veal Milanese, 88
Vegetables. *See also specific*
  vegetables
  freezing, 9
  frozen mixed, 12
  Vegetable Kebabs, 67
  Vegetable Minestrone, 24
Vinegars, 13

W
Walnuts
  Creamy Gnocchi with
    Gorgonzola and
    Walnuts, 42–43
  Stuffed Mushroom Caps, 64
White Peach and Raspberry
  Bellini, 107
Wine (Italian)
  Asti Spumante, 14
  Barbera, 15
  Chianti, 15
  Lemon and Mint Sgroppino, 108
  Pinot Grigio, 14
  reds, 15
  Sangiovese, 15
  Sauvignon Blanc, 14
  Soave, 14
  White Peach and Raspberry
    Bellini, 107
  whites, 14
Wooden spoons, 16

Z
Ziti con Funghi Cremini, 74
Zucchini, 7
  Rigatoni with Vegetarian Ragù, 48
  Scapece-Style Zucchini, 62
  Vegetable Kebabs, 67
Zucchini alla Scapece, 62
Zuppa Imperiale, 28

ACKNOWLEDGMENTS

To my mom, Celeste Montillo, whom I treasure dearly and who is my constant culinary critic, making me a better home cook in the process—thank you for your direction, in life and in the kitchen. To my sister, Roseanne Montillo, who years ago insisted I write a cookbook. Now, three books later, none of them would have been possible without your initial nudge.

And a big *thank you* to my Zoom culinary students. I never would have thought I would be teaching cooking over Zoom, but the pandemic pushed my business that way, and I never would have known the hundreds of students I have had the privilege of meeting if not for this method of teaching. So thank you to all of you, from the bottom of my heart.

ABOUT THE AUTHOR

FRANCESCA MONTILLO is the author of *The Five-Ingredient Italian Cookbook* (Rockridge Press, 2018) and *Pasta in a Pinch* (Rockridge Press, 2020). She is also the owner of Lazy Italian Culinary Adventures. Combining the two things she adores the most, Francesca is now a culinary instructor (in person and over Zoom) and a culinary tour leader in Italy. Via her classes and team-building events, she teaches her students recipes that are uncomplicated, straightforward, and easily replicated at home. Via her tours, she brings people to the source, Italy, to learn about Italian food and wine. For information on her cooking classes or culinary adventures to Italy, you can visit Francesca at thelazyitalian.com.

CPSIA information can be obtained
at www.ICGtesting.com
Printed in the USA
JSHW011104280921
19063JS00002B/8